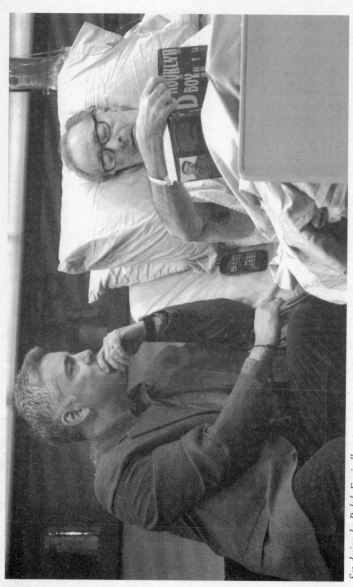

Adam Arkin and Allan Miller in a scene from the New York production of *Brooklyn Boy.*

BROOKLYN BOY

BOY

BY DONALD MARGULIES

★

DRAMATISTS
PLAY SERVICE
INC.

INTRODUCTION

Herb Gardner urged me to go back.

The author of the plays *I'm Not Rappaport* and *Conversations with My Father*, who died in 2003 at sixty-eight after a tenacious struggle with emphysema, was my friend. A couple of years ago, he and I were having one of our marathon phone conversations, he at home on the Upper East Side, I in my office in New Haven, Connecticut, when I confided in him the difficulty I was having in starting a new play. I was in my mid-forties, coming down from the headiness of the biggest success of my career and suffering from a severe case of: "Now what?"

"I love your Brooklyn plays," he said. "Why don't you go back to Brooklyn?"

"I don't *want* to go back to Brooklyn," I told him. "It took me years to get out of Brooklyn, why would I want to go back now?"

"Because you've never looked at it from this point in your life before."

Herb was right. I had tilled the soil of my Brooklyn-Jewish upbringing in a succession of semi-autobiographical plays written during the '70s and '80s but had consciously steered clear of Brooklyn ever since. Retrospectively, there is a *bildungsroman* progression to these plays: *Found a Peanut* (1984), set in the concrete backyard of a Brooklyn apartment building on the last day of the summer of 1962, was a snapshot of childhood; *The Loman Family Picnic* (1989), centered on a nouveau-middle-class Brooklyn family's tragicomically desperate handling of its firstborn son's bar mitzvah; and *What's Wrong with This Picture?* (1985), in which an adolescent reeling from his mother's sudden death is confronted by the dead woman herself, who has come back on the last night of shiva to clean their Flatbush apartment.

While the focus of my 1991 play *Sight Unseen* was no longer on a Jewish son but on a mature Jewish artist, and the drama was set mostly in England, the play still had a foot—and, arguably, its heart—in Brooklyn. The play served effectively as a bridge between the provincial Brooklyn of my youth and the outside world; it also proved to be the career breakthrough that enriched my life in many ways, not the least of which was that it provided the catalyst for my friendship with Herb Gardner.

Shortly after *Sight Unseen* premiered in New York at Manhattan Theatre Club in 1992 (it originated the previous year at South Coast Repertory), I was invited to write a piece for the *New York Times*. The essay, "A Playwright's Search for the Spiritual Father" (which ran on Father's Day), was a rumination on fathers and mentors, creativity and influence. In it, I described the seminal experience, at age eight, of seeing my first Broadway play. The play that had me utterly transfixed was *A Thousand Clowns*; the playwright was Herb Gardner.

A few days after the article ran, I received a note from a man I'd never met: "What, here it is Sunday and you don't give your spiritual father a call?" The writer of the note, of course, was Herb, and, fatefully, he included his telephone number. I called him, we met, and I instantly acquired a new old friend, one with whom I would commiserate, kvetch and laugh, over meals and, as his disease progressed, increasingly over the phone, for the next decade.

I can't muse about Brooklyn without thinking about Herb. We were both Brooklyn boys, although he was nearly a generation older; Herb's Brooklyn was my parents' Brooklyn. Theirs was the real thing, the Brooklyn of legend, not the faded, ghostly place where baby boomers like me grew up.

My parents met at a block party in Flatbush on V-J Day. Their wartime courtship took on an iconic quality in my imagination, as if they were stars of their own Warner Brothers picture, set to a Big Band score.

My fantasy was fed by movies of that era that mythologized Brooklyn and made archetypes of its people, all of them blunt, unpretentious, salt-of-the-earth, who spoke a kind of roughhewn poetry. War movies always seemed to include lovable, vaguely Jewish GIs who hailed from or were even called "Brooklyn" and who would no doubt be dead by the final reel. Family photos from the '40s pictured preternaturally mature bobby-soxers with lipstick and cigarettes, seemingly all of them resembling Olivia de Havilland or Linda Darnell.

To have come of age in Eisenhower-era, baby-boomer Brooklyn was to feel cheated of the glory days. The Dodgers had already moved west; Ebbets Field was leveled and replaced with a high-rise housing project. Steeplechase Park in Coney Island shut its doors when I was ten; I was there exactly once, shortly before it closed, and still recall my one exhilarating spin down its burnished mahogany slide.

By the late '60s, public school education, which had served me and my fellow boomers so well for a time, was no longer a panacea for upwardly mobile middle-class kids. The families of those kids moved upward—or outward—to the suburban promise of Long Island and sent once-solid Brooklyn neighborhoods spiraling downward.

Once urban flight took hold, the last vestiges of my parents' Brooklyn vanished. Streets and subways were no longer safe. The Sheepshead movie theater was converted into a roller-skating rink; the Elm Theatre became a bank. Ebinger's Bakery, famous for its chocolate blackout cakes, went out of business and Dubrow's Cafeteria, best known for its kasha varnishkas, closed its revolving doors.

If I long for Brooklyn it is not so much for the geographical place where I spent my childhood but for an ethos that was already dead or dying by the time I was old enough to realize that something was amiss. When I look back at Brooklyn now, from the vantage point of the middle of my life, I find that it is a place that no longer exists, indeed one that may never have truly existed in my lifetime. Maybe it's because I no longer have a familial connection to the place; my parents are long gone and my brother has moved to L.A. Maybe it's a feeling I've always had. I was nostalgic for my parents' and Herb Gardner's Brooklyn ever since I was a boy.

When I was growing up in Sheepshead Bay and Coney Island in the '50s and '60s, the Brooklyn Bridge took on for me almost mystical significance. That exquisite span was the gateway to a gleaming city where the future was bound to be more exciting than that which lay ahead in Brooklyn. In my young, television-addled mind, the New York skyline had merged with that of the Emerald City, a magical notion fed by repeated annual viewings of *The Wizard of Oz*. Manhattan was a place rendered in vivid Technicolor while Brooklyn's hue was not even black-and-white but drab sepia.

Perhaps it is the omnipresence of that majestic bridge and those shimmering skyscrapers that contribute to the Brooklynite's perpetual state of self-consciousness, for those landmarks are constant reminders of his marginal place in the world. The Brooklynite lives on the periphery, tantalizingly within reach of Something Else, Something Greater, lying just across the river. It is precisely that condition which shapes personalities, fuels ambitions, and creates in some an overwhelming sense of restlessness and yearning.

Brooklyn is the metaphoric home to anyone who has ever seen himself as an outsider, who has ever been torn between the powerful, atavistic tug toward the traditional and familiar and the magnetic allure of the unknown.

Brooklyn is the past recorded in faded Super 8. It is innocence, childhood, family, community, a safe place. Brooklyn is Rosebud, Camelot, Atlantis. It is the state of grace that exists solely in memory or fantasy. Brooklyn is the precious thing we've lost.

So when my friend called me back to Brooklyn that day on the phone, I followed, with all the queasy curiosity of a prodigal son looking homeward. I knew the terrain well but hadn't walked it as a man in midlife. Scenes began to lay themselves out; I started to get a sense of the landscape of a new play. It would not be a sentimental journey bathed in nostalgia, but a fresh exploration of old themes, clear-eyed and present tense. If *Sight Unseen* was a play about leaving Brooklyn, then *Brooklyn Boy* would be one about looking back.

In 1994 *What's Wrong with This Picture?* opened on Broadway. As the actors took their curtain call, two huge hands grasped my shoulders in triumph. It was Herb, seated in the row behind me. How fitting that the man who was largely responsible for my early infatuation with theater should be present on the night of my Broadway debut, literally right behind me, cheering me on. In a sense, Herb, the über Brooklyn boy, was there all along.

This play is for him.

—Donald Margulies
New Haven, Connecticut

This essay first appeared in the Los Angeles *Times* on Sunday, September 5, 2004.

BROOKLYN BOY was originally co-produced by South Coast Repertory (David Emmes, Producing Artistic Director; Martin Benson, Artistic Director; Paula Tomei, Managing Director) and Manhattan Theatre Club (Lynne Meadow, Artistic Director; Barry Grove, Executive Producer) and received its world premiere at South Coast Repertory in Costa Mesa, California, on September 3, 2004. It was directed by Daniel Sullivan; the set design was by Ralph Funicello; the costume design was by Jess Goldstein; the lighting design was by Chris Parry; the original music and sound design were by Michael Roth; the dramaturg was Jerry Patch; and the stage manager was Scott Harrison. The cast was as follows:

ERIC WEISS .... Adam Arkin
MANNY WEISS .... Allan Miller
IRA ZIMMER .... Arye Gross
NINA .... Dana Reeve
ALISON .... Ari Graynor
MELANIE FINE .... Mimi Lieber
TYLER SHAW .... Kevin Isola

BROOKLYN BOY opened on Broadway at Manhattan Theatre Club's Biltmore Theatre on February 3, 2005, with the following changes: Polly Draper played the part of Nina, and the production stage manager was Roy Harris.

CHARACTERS

ERIC WEISS, a novelist, mid-forties

MANNY WEISS, his father, seventy

IRA ZIMMER, Eric's childhood friend, mid-forties

NINA, Eric's wife, forties

ALISON, a college student, twenties

MELANIE FINE, a film producer, late thirties

TYLER SHAW, a movie star, early twenties

PLACE

Brooklyn, the East Village, and Los Angeles.

TIME

The present.

BROOKLYN BOY

ACT ONE

Scene 1

Maimonides

A room in Maimonides Hospital, Brooklyn. Ambient sounds. The wall-mounted television is on, its back to the audience, the soundtrack of an old movie barely audible. Manny Weiss dozes in a hospital bed. His breathing is labored. He is ill; several IVs are attached. His son, Eric, dressed casually but well, carrying a hardcover book, the Daily News *and the* New York Post, *enters and watches him breathe. He drapes his coat and umbrella over a chair, puts his gifts on the crank table beside an abandoned food tray, and sits. He watches the movie on TV. Soon Manny awakens and sees Eric.*

MANNY. Jesus, I must be sicker than I thought.
ERIC. Hi.
MANNY. *(Sits up with effort; disoriented.)* What time is it?
ERIC. *(Looks at his watch.)* 2:43.
MANNY. Day or night?
ERIC. Day.
MANNY. How long you been sitting there?
ERIC. Not long. How long have you been sleeping?
MANNY. I wasn't sleeping; I was just closing my eyes.
ERIC. Uh-huh.
MANNY. Fix me. *(Meaning his position. Eric raises the bed electronically and puffs up pillows to prop up Manny.)* Higher. Lower. *Lower.* Uh! *(Meaning, "Stop!")*
ERIC. Better?

9

MANNY. I don't know. Leave it, the hell with it. Thought you were out of town.

ERIC. I was. I was in Miami.

MANNY. Can't keep track of you. When'd you get back?

ERIC. Last night. And I'm leaving again tomorrow.

MANNY. Again?!

ERIC. *(Nods, then.)* Tomorrow I go to L.A. I wanted to see you.

MANNY. *(Sarcastic.)* All the way to Brooklyn just to see *me?* Gee, I'm honored. Your wife with you?

ERIC. No.

MANNY. I never see her — Nina. She's always busy.

ERIC. She *is* busy. She sends her best, though.

MANNY. That's nice. *(A beat.)* Got any good news for me?

ERIC. What kind of good news?

MANNY. *You* know.

ERIC. *(A beat.)* No. No good news.

MANNY. Thought maybe I had something to look forward to.

ERIC. *(Regarding the TV.)* What *movie* is this?

MANNY. What?

ERIC. I'm trying to figure out what movie this is. Ronald Colman, Shelley Winters …

MANNY. Don't ask *me.* It was black-and-white, I left it on. *(Silence as they both watch.)*

ERIC. *A Double Life? (Manny shrugs.)* I think it *is.* Ronald Colman's an actor playing Othello who starts confusing the role with real life? *(Manny shrugs. They watch.)* See? She's his Desdemona.

MANNY. His what?

ERIC. Never mind. Haven't you been watching it?

MANNY. I've been *look*ing at it, yeah; that doesn't mean I've been paying at*ten*tion. *(Eric turns it off.)* Hey!

ERIC. You said you weren't watching it.

MANNY. I did *not* say that! Turn it back on!

ERIC. Okay! *(Turns it back on.)*

MANNY. I *like* having it on. It gives me something to look at.

ERIC. Well, *excuse* me. Mind if I mute it at least? I don't like having to compete with the television.

MANNY. Do what you want. As long as you leave the picture. *(Stays fixed on the silent image.)*

ERIC. So? How're you feeling? *(Manny shrugs.)* How was your night?

MANNY. Terrific.

ERIC. Really?

10

MANNY. No. What do you think? It's like Klein's basement in here. Nurses in and out all night long — you should see what goes on here!

ERIC. Has the doctor been in to see you today?

MANNY. Which doctor?

ERIC. Dr. Patel?

MANNY. Which one is he?

ERIC. The oncologist.

MANNY. The Indian guy?

ERIC. Yeah. Has he been here today?

MANNY. I don't know. Last night, maybe? This morning? Who can keep track?

ERIC. I thought if he was around ... I thought maybe I could talk to him. *(Manny shrugs dismissively. Pause.)*

MANNY. What's it doing out there? Still raining?

ERIC. Stopped.

MANNY. Boy. It was really coming down before.

ERIC. *(Nods, then:)* I brought you the papers. You want to look at the papers?

MANNY. *(Over " ... at the papers?")* Nah.

ERIC. You sure?

MANNY. Words are too much. Can't concentrate.

ERIC. I'll leave them right here. How's that? In case you change your mind. *(Manny shrugs. Silence. Eric looks over the food tray.)* You didn't eat much lunch. *(Manny makes a disgusted sound.)* You didn't want your chocolate pudding?

MANNY. Tastes like chalk.

ERIC. It looks fine.

MANNY. Then *you* eat it.

ERIC. *(He does, makes a face.)* Uch.

MANNY. *(Amused.)* See? You didn't believe me.

ERIC. Want an orange? Not too much they can do to an orange. *(Manny shakes his head.)* You want some?

MANNY. Can't. I got these sores. *(In his mouth.)*

ERIC. *(Hands him a section.)* Come on, you've got to eat *some*-thing. It's vitamin C. It's good for canker sores. Here.

MANNY. *(Takes it.)* I don't like the stringy part.

ERIC. I'll peel *off* the stringy part. *(He does. Pause.)* Has Aunt Rose been to see you?

MANNY. *(Shrugs; his eyes on the TV.)* She comes.

ERIC. And?

11

MANNY. And nothing. She sits, she cries, she goes.

ERIC. So. Dad. This book tour.

MANNY. Miami you said?

ERIC. Miami, Sunrise, West Palm Beach …

MANNY. What for?

ERIC. Book signings.

MANNY. All those places book signings?

ERIC. Uh-huh.

MANNY. What happens?

ERIC. I read an excerpt, a selection, and then I sign books.

MANNY. That's what you do? You sit there and sign books?

ERIC. Basically.

MANNY. And people buy them from you?

ERIC. From the bookstore, yeah; I don't actually collect the money.

MANNY. And people really come to these things?

ERIC. Yeah.

MANNY. Like how many?

ERIC. Depends. This Jewish center outside of Cleveland last week? Maybe twenty …

MANNY. That's not very much.

ERIC. Yeah, but the other day at a bookstore in Miami, over two hundred showed up.

MANNY. Two hundred people bought your book?!

ERIC. No, that's how many came to hear me read. Maybe forty bought the book. Forty or fifty.

MANNY. Yeah? And that's good?

ERIC. For a serious novel? It's not bad.

MANNY. What do you mean by serious?

ERIC. Not schlock. A literary novel. A book that aspires to be literature.

MANNY. Oh, well, hoity-toity.

ERIC. *(A beat.)* Did you, uh, happen to catch the *Today* show the other day?

MANNY. No, I missed it. I know you told me …

ERIC. *(Over "I know … ")* That's okay.

MANNY. Your aunt saw it, though.

ERIC. Oh, yeah? What'd she say?

MANNY. She said why didn't you wear a tie.

ERIC. That's all she said?

MANNY. She said you looked tired. And you should've worn a tie.

ERIC. I was supposed to look like a serious writer.

MANNY. What, serious writers don't wear ties? I didn't know that. You see the president running around without a tie?

ERIC. The president isn't a serious writer. *(Eric feeds him the orange.)*

MANNY. Mmm.

ERIC. Good? *(Manny nods.)* More? *(Manny nods. Eric feeds him.)*

MANNY. So don't you gotta get up early for that?

ERIC. For what?

MANNY. The *Today* show thing.

ERIC. Four-thirty.

MANNY. Four-thirty in the morning?!

ERIC. Uh-huh. They sent a car.

MANNY. What kind of car?

ERIC. A Town Car.

MANNY. A *Town* Car? Really? Just for you?

ERIC. Just for me.

MANNY. Wow. A Lincoln all to yourself? They could've paid your cab fare, it would've been cheaper. They feed you breakfast?

ERIC. Oh yeah. In the greenroom. Backstage. *You* know.

MANNY. Like what?

ERIC. Coffee and bagels. Doughnuts.

MANNY. Danish?

ERIC. Uh-huh.

MANNY. Buffet-style? All you can eat?

ERIC. Yeah.

MANNY. You go back for seconds?

ERIC. No.

MANNY. Why not? All that free food?! What are *they* gonna do with it?

ERIC. I was a little nervous; I wasn't very hungry.

MANNY. So what do you do there all that time?

ERIC. They brief you, they put on makeup …

MANNY. You put on *make*up?

ERIC. Yeah.

MANNY. You did? Couldn't you refuse?

ERIC. They do it so you don't look pale on camera.

MANNY. Your aunt said you looked pale anyway. They couldn't lend you a tie while they were at it?

ERIC. I didn't *want* to wear a tie. I wore a nice pullover; I thought I looked good. I could get you a tape if you'd like.

MANNY. How'm I supposed to watch it?

ERIC. Don't they have VCRs here?

MANNY. Here? It's a hospital, not a hotel.

ERIC. I'll bet they do. They must. If you want me to look into it, I will. *(Manny shrugs.)* Okay? I'll ask on my way out. *(Manny gestures disinterestedly.)* I thought you might get a kick out of seeing your son talking to Katie Couric on national television. That's all.

MANNY. Is that who you talked to? Katie Couric?

ERIC. Uh-huh.

MANNY. The little one? Perky-like?

ERIC. Yeah.

MANNY. Jane *Pauley* I liked. When *she* left, it all went downhill from there. *(Eric gives him the book.)* What's this?

ERIC. It's for *you.*

MANNY. My glasses … *(Eric finds the glasses and hands them to him. Manny reads the cover:)* Brooklyn Boy. Well! How do you like that! By Eric Weiss. So this is it.

ERIC. This is it.

MANNY. Look how fat it is! Wow. *(Hefts it.)* It's so heavy! How many pages?

ERIC. Not that many; 384.

MANNY. 384! That's a lot!

ERIC. Not really.

MANNY. 384? What do you have to say that would take 384 pages?

ERIC. You'd be surprised, it just …

MANNY. *(Looks at author's photo.)* Who's this? That supposed to be *you?* Gee, it's such a good-looking picture I almost didn't recognize you.

ERIC. Thanks.

MANNY. Who took the picture?

ERIC. Nina.

MANNY. Very nice. Put this over there will you please?

ERIC. Wait, I want to show you something. *(Eric turns to the dedication page and shows it to him. Manny reads it:)*

MANNY. "For my mother and my father." *(Pause.)* That mean me and your mother?

ERIC. Yeah.

MANNY. *(Nods, then.)* Where's our names?

ERIC. What do you mean?

MANNY. Don't we get our names? Couldn't you say: "For Phyllis and Manny Weiss"? Then there wouldn't be any confusion.

ERIC. *What* confusion? There *is* no confusion.

MANNY. This could be *any*body's mother and father.

ERIC. It says "*my* mother and father." It's *my* book.

MANNY. You couldn't've put in a little plug for me and your mother?

ERIC. A little *plug?*

MANNY. It would've given your mother may she rest in peace such *nakhess* to see her name in print. When do people like us ever get to do that? Huh? When we *die*; that's about it. *(Holds out the book.)* Stick it over there.

ERIC. *(Incredulous.)* Dad, I dedicated my *book* to you. This is my *book*.

MANNY. I *know* it's your book.

ERIC. I worked on this book for years; you know I did.

MANNY. So?

ERIC. So?! *This* is what I've been *do*ing. It's been six years between books. And here it is. Finally. Dad: It's a bestseller. First time in my life. This Sunday: *Brooklyn Boy* is number eleven.

MANNY. How do *you* know?

ERIC. I know; my publisher told me.

MANNY. How does *he* know? Sunday paper's not out yet.

ERIC. The trade finds out in advance.

MANNY. *Eleven?*

ERIC. Yes.

MANNY. You mean there *is* an eleven? I thought it only went to ten.

ERIC. No, it goes to fifteen.

MANNY. Since when?

ERIC. Since, I don't know, since several years ago.

MANNY. Huh. I thought it only went to ten.

ERIC. No.

MANNY. Wow, good thing they made the list longer. Lucky for you, huh?

ERIC. *(Disappointed.)* Yeah. *(A beat.)* Do you have any idea what this means?

MANNY. What.

ERIC. This is potentially life-changing. Do you realize that? After all these years? I've broken through, Dad. And I'd really appreciate it if you looked at it for more than two seconds.

MANNY. I *did* look at it; I *looked* at it.

ERIC. *(Over " … at it.")* Never mind.

MANNY. What do you want from me?

ERIC. I want you to *read* it.

MANNY. *Now?*

ERIC. Of course not *now.*

MANNY. *(Continuous.)* I'd hate to do that to you; I'm a very slow reader.

ERIC. I want you to pretend that it means something to you. That's all. Just pretend.

MANNY. *(Over "Just pretend.")* Means something to me?

ERIC. Yes.

MANNY. What do you mean, *means* something?

ERIC. *Means* something! Has significance to you!

MANNY. *(Overlapping.)* Shhhh. You gonna *yell* at me now?

ERIC. *(More controlled.)* This isn't just an ordinary book somebody brought you. Do you understand that?

MANNY. No, I'm very stupid.

ERIC. It's your son's book. Something your son made.

MANNY. You didn't "make" it. You made the binding? *(Eric, disgusted, gets his coat. Manny extends his hand.)* Hey. *(Pause.)* Hey. Give me the book. Give it to me! *(Eric hands the book back to him. Pause.)* You *know* reading's not my thing.

ERIC. I *do* know that.

MANNY. 380-odd pages, that's a hell of a lot to ask from somebody like me.

ERIC. I know.

MANNY. I can't make any promises.

ERIC. I understand.

MANNY. If I have the time …

ERIC. What do you *mean* if you have the time, you've got a pressing engagement I don't know about?

MANNY. Ha ha. *(A beat.)* I tried reading those *other* books of yours, you know Those *first* two.

ERIC. I know.

MANNY. *The Something Something* and that other one. *The…?*

ERIC. *The Gentleman Farmer* and *The Aerie.*

MANNY. The what?

ERIC. *The Aerie.*

MANNY. *The Aerie.* Right. *The Aerie.* I still have no idea what the hell an "aerie" *is* …

ERIC. Yes you do. I've told you many times: an aerie is a bird's nest.

MANNY. Then why couldn't you call it *The Bird's Nest*? I don't understand that! Something people could pronounce. No wonder nobody bought it; they didn't know how to ask for it.

16

ERIC. People bought it, just not in very high numbers.

MANNY. And what do you know from "gentlemen farmers"?

ERIC. It's a metaphoric title.

MANNY. A what?

ERIC. Nothing.

MANNY. So it's about Brooklyn, this one?

ERIC. It's set here, yeah.

MANNY. See? That's why it's popular. Didn't I tell you to write something popular?

ERIC. You did?

MANNY. Yes I did. You don't remember but I certainly did. You should do very well with this one. A lot of people come from Brooklyn. They can relate. Birds' nests, farmers: Who gives a shit?

ERIC. It takes place in the sixties and seventies. When I was growing up. You'll recognize a lot of it.

MANNY. Oh, yeah? Like Ebbets Field, Sheepshead Bay?

ERIC. Sort of. I mean you'll recognize the people.

MANNY. Oh, you mean like famous Brooklynites?

ERIC. No.

MANNY. Barbra Streisand? She's from Brooklyn, you know.

ERIC. I know. No, not Barbra Streisand.

MANNY. Did I ever tell you Neil Sedaka's parents had a hot dog stand in Brighton?

ERIC. Yeah, you did.

MANNY. Just as you got on the boardwalk. Right on the ramp …

ERIC. Uh-huh.

MANNY. … There was Sedaka's. I remember him as a kid. Did you know I knew him as a kid?

ERIC. Yes; I did.

MANNY. Did you know Lauren Bacall is Jewish?

ERIC. Uh-huh.

MANNY. Isn't that unbelievable?

ERIC. Not really. Dad, what I meant was you'll recognize the characters. *(A beat.)* It's about a family.

MANNY. Who.

ERIC. People like us.

MANNY. Like "us" us?

ERIC. Uh-huh.

MANNY. Uh-oh. Am *I* in it?

ERIC. Uh-huh. Kinda.

MANNY. Yeah? Is your mother?

ERIC. Oh, yeah.

MANNY. By *name*?

ERIC. No. When I say you're in it, I mean there are things about the father that are a lot *like* you. But it's *not* you.

MANNY. What's his name?

ERIC. Arnie Fleischman.

MANNY. Arnie Fleischman instead of Manny Weiss?

ERIC. Uh-huh.

MANNY. Fleischman was your mother's maiden name, you know.

ERIC. I know.

MANNY. And what does Arnie Fleischman do for a living? Sell shoes like me?

ERIC. No; he's a barber.

MANNY. *(Disapproving.)* He doesn't work in a *beauty* parlor …

ERIC. No; he works in a barber shop. He cuts men's hair.

MANNY. Good; 'cause "beauty parlor," automatically you think … *(A beat.)* What's *your* name in it?

ERIC. The *son's* name is Kenny.

MANNY. Kenny Fleischman? Kenny Fleischman instead of Ricky Weiss?

ERIC. Uh-huh.

MANNY. *(Flips through pages.)* Are there any pictures?

ERIC. No, Dad, it's not an autobiography, it's a novel.

MANNY. What does *that* mean? I don't understand the difference.

ERIC. *(Over " … the difference.")* It means it's a story. It's made up.

MANNY. I thought you said it was us.

ERIC. They're *like* us. They're *inspired* by us.

MANNY. Now you lost me.

ERIC. They're people *like* us …

MANNY. But not us.

ERIC. Right.

MANNY. In other words, it's *not* the Weiss family of Ocean Avenue.

ERIC. Right. The Fleischmans live on Nostrand.

MANNY. So that's what you did? You called us the Fleischmans and moved us to Nostrand Avenue?

ERIC. Yeah …

MANNY. And that makes it a novel?

ERIC. Well, not just that.

MANNY. Gee, *I* should write a novel.

ERIC. Go right ahead.

MANNY. Watch out, I might make it to number one.

ERIC. Great; I hope you do. So, remember, not everything in the book actually happened.

MANNY. But some of it did?

ERIC. Yeah.

MANNY. So is there stuff in here I'm not gonna like?

ERIC. I don't know. I hope not.

MANNY. 'Cause I don't care what you say about *me* but your *mothe*r … I don't want you saying anything nasty about your mother.

ERIC. What makes you think I'd be nasty?

MANNY. It isn't nice, when a person can't defend herself. Is *your* wife in here, too, or her you let off easy.

ERIC. No, a character based on Nina comes in later, toward the end. Look, you're just gonna have to read it and see for yourself.

MANNY. I will. I'll give you a full report.

ERIC. Good.

MANNY. How's that? I'll give you a review.

ERIC. Great. I'm anxious to hear what you think.

MANNY. *(A warning.)* I can be a pretty tough critic, you know.

ERIC. Believe me, I know. *(Manny turns his attention to the TV. Eric watches him. Silence.)* Dad, what are you thinking about these days?

MANNY. What do you *mean* what am I thinking about?

ERIC. You've been lying here with all this time to think. What's been going through your mind?

MANNY. How the hell do *I* know?

ERIC. Any Big Thoughts? *(A beat.)* Have you been thinking a lot about Mom?

MANNY. My eyes hurt. Do me a favor, turn down the light. *(Eric turns off the overhead light.)*

ERIC. Dad, we have to talk about what happens when you leave the hospital.

MANNY. I'm not *leaving* the hospital.

ERIC. What do you mean?

MANNY. I'm not leaving the *hos*pital. This is it this time.

ERIC. How do *you* know?

MANNY. I *know. (Pause. Off the TV:)* Oh, look! Look who that is! That's whatshername!

ERIC. Shelley Winters.

MANNY. Who?

ERIC. Shelley Winters.

MANNY. *That's* right! Boy, look how young and thin she was! Look at her! She was beautiful! *(A beat.)* I tell ya, Ricky, time is the worst damn thing in the world. *(Eric looks at his father, then at the TV.)*

Scene 2

Cafeteria

Later that afternoon. The commissary in the lobby of the hospital. Ambient sounds: pages for doctors, din, easy-listening Muzak. Eric, seated with a cup of coffee, punches in a number on his cell phone, waits, then leaves a message. Ira Zimmer, Eric's age, although he looks older, rumpled, soft, wearing a yarmulke, enters holding a tray with a cup of coffee and a wedge of layer cake, and sits one table away from Eric. He reads a discarded newspaper and glances at Eric, who looks familiar.

ERIC. *(Into his phone.)* Hi, Nina, it's me. The Prodigal Returneth. Listen, I got your message. I thought maybe I could stop by *tonight,* if that's all right, and get that stuff out of your way. I'm in Brooklyn right now, still at the hospital. I could probably make it home by … *(A small laugh.)* — I mean to *your* place — let's say around six. How's that? Call me if that's a problem, otherwise I'll see you then. Okay? Um … *(Eric and Zimmer briefly make eye contact; he ends his call.)* See you later.
ZIMMER. *(Incredulously.)* Ricky?
ERIC. Yes?
ZIMMER. Ricky Weiss, Eric Weiss, the *writer* Eric Weiss?
ERIC. Yes? …
ZIMMER. Oh my God, this is so weird, I was just talking about you!
ERIC. You were?
ZIMMER. It's *beshert.* You know what that means, *beshert?*
ERIC. Yes.
ZIMMER. Meant to be. Fate.
ERIC. I know.
ZIMMER. *Look* at you, *you* look exactly the same, *me* I turn into

20

my father. (*Eric chuckles, wondering, Who* is *this guy?*)

ERIC. Do we know each other?

ZIMMER. Do we *know* each other?! Do we *KNOW* each other?!

ERIC. (*Over "Do we KNOW ... "*) I'm sorry ...

ZIMMER. What, you're too famous to remember your old buddy, Zimmer?!

ERIC. Ira?!

ZIMMER. Yes, Mr. Big Shot! Mr. Famous!

ERIC. (*Over "Mr. Famous!"*) Ira Zimmer! (*They shake hands.*) I didn't recognize you!

ZIMMER. No kidding!

ERIC. I mean out of context.

ZIMMER. What "out of context"? This is Brooklyn! This *is* the context!

ERIC. I never expected to run into anyone I knew here.

ZIMMER. Maimonides Hospital? You thought you were safe? *Every*body passes through here sooner or later. It's the last stop for Brooklyn Jews. Who you got here?

ERIC. My father.

ZIMMER. Bad?

ERIC. Pretty bad, yeah. You?

ZIMMER. My mom. Also bad.

ERIC. I'm sorry to hear that. Is your dad...?

ZIMMER. Dead.

ERIC. Oh, gee, I'm sorry.

ZIMMER. (*Shrugs.*) Long time ago; what can ya do. He was on my case about *ev*erything, that mean sonofabitch asshole may he rest in peace.

ERIC. You *do* look like him.

ZIMMER. I know, isn't it freaky? I freak my*self* out sometimes. *Look* at this. (*Rolls up his sleeves.*) These are his forearms! How did *his* forearms end up on *my* body? — Your dad must be, what?, like seventy-something now?

ERIC. Seventy, exactly.

ZIMMER. Wow. Seventy. My mom's seventy-three.

ERIC. Amazing. I remember her when she was our age. She must've been around our age when we were bar mitzvahed, right?

ZIMMER. Younger, even.

ERIC. I remember her lipstick-red hair done up in a sweep.

ZIMMER. Yeah. Not much of *that* left. Chemo.

ERIC. My dad, too. Prostate. Metastatic.

ZIMMER. Uy.

ERIC. It's in his spine, it's everywhere.

ZIMMER. Uch, terrible. My mom? Ovarian.

ERIC. Jeez that's a bad one.

ZIMMER. Let's face it, they're all bad, all of 'em.

ERIC. True. *(A beat.)* You know what threw me? The yarmulke!

ZIMMER. Oh, yeah? My little *kippah?* I guess I got a little Ortho-
dox since the last time you saw me.

ERIC. *(Over " … you saw me.")* "A little"? Is that like being a little
pregnant? Since when did you get so *frum? (Devout.)*

ZIMMER. Since Mindy Goldberg.

ERIC. *(That explains it.)* Ah! I *see* …

ZIMMER. Went to my temple's singles group hoping to meet a
nice Jewish girl? Didn't mean one *this* Jewish. *(Handles the yarmulke.)* My daughter made me this.

ERIC. You have a daughter?

ZIMMER. Bubbie, I have *three* daughters.

ERIC. Three?!

ZIMMER. *And* a son.

ERIC. Wow!

ZIMMER. And one on the way.

ERIC. Jesus, Ira, isn't that going a little overboard?

ZIMMER. What can I tell ya? When it comes to procreation, we're
worse than Catholics. My daughter Sara made this. *(His yarmulke.)*

ERIC. Nice.

ZIMMER. Didn't she do a nice job?

ERIC. Lovely. How old is she?

ZIMMER. Twelve.

ERIC. Twelve?! You have a *twelve*-year old?! How can that be?! To
me you're still thirteen.

ZIMMER. I know. Want to hear something even scarier than my
having a twelve year old? I have a *sixteen*-year old.

ERIC. Wow, that *is* scary. *(Zimmer takes out his wallet and moves
to the table adjacent to Eric.)*

ZIMMER. *(Shows photos.)* Leah, Aviva, Sara and Ari.

ERIC. Look at that!

ZIMMER. *(Continuous.)* Sixteen, fourteen, twelve and nine.

ERIC. They look great, Ira. Great-looking kids.

ZIMMER. Thousands of bucks in orthodontia right there.
(Another photo.) And there's my Mindy. Yup, there she is. The
things we do for love, huh?

ERIC. Wonderful family. *Mazel tov.*

ZIMMER. *(Puts his wallet back.)* Look, it's a life. Hey, you mind if I, uh … *(Meaning, join him.)*

ERIC. Yeah, sure, why not?

ZIMMER. *(Over " … why not?"; moves his tray over.)* I gotta eat something, I'm famished — not to be confused with *famisht.* You can use that line if you want; I give you permission. So who do you see?

ERIC. Who do I see?

ZIMMER. From the old days. Hirsch? Weinberg?

ERIC. No. No one really.

ZIMMER. Sarokin?

ERIC. No.

ZIMMER. Wow. Not even Sarokin? *(Eric shakes his head.)* Boy! And you guys were like so …

ERIC. I know.

ZIMMER. I was always so jealous. Hey, we should all get together!

ERIC. Uh-huh.

ZIMMER. Wouldn't that be a gas?!

ERIC. Yeah.

ZIMMER. I'll organize a reunion! I'm always running into kids from back then. "Kids." *Lis*ten to me! They're middle-aged people! — You got kids?

ERIC. No.

ZIMMER. No?! What're you waiting for?! *(His mouth full.)* Want some?

ERIC. *(Realizing he means cake.)* Oh, no, no thanks.

ZIMMER. *(Half joking.)* Good; I didn't want to give you anyway. What's your wife's name?

ERIC. Nina.

ZIMMER. She Jewish?

ERIC. No.

ZIMMER. *(A concession.)* All right. What does she do?

ERIC. She's a wonderful writer.

ZIMMER. Two writers. What's *that* like?

ERIC. Interesting. Hey, do you still draw?

ZIMMER. Me? Nah. Sometimes I'll doodle something for the kids.

ERIC. I remember the comic book heroes you created. They were terrific.

ZIMMER. Yeah, yeah. I decided long ago, back in high school: *You* can be the famous one. My mom and I were just saying what a big *macher* you are.

ERIC. Believe me, Ira, I'm no *macher.*

ZIMMER. Whataya talking about? I saw you on TV!

ERIC. You saw that?

ZIMMER. Me and several million *other* people, yeah. I'm sitting there eating breakfast … *(Announcer voice.)* "In the next half hour … Eric Weiss, author of *Brooklyn Boy* … "

ERIC. Oh, God.

ZIMMER. I almost choked on my Cheerios! *(Eric laughs.)* I swear: *Milk* almost came shooting out of my *nose!* You were great!

ERIC. Thanks.

ZIMMER. So cool, so relaxed! Like you've been doing this your whole life! Mindy was impressed; she thought you were cute.

ERIC. Oh, yeah?

ZIMMER. *(Pinches his cheek.) Shayna punim!* If you didn't sell a million books that day! … You're all over the place! I'm at my *dentist's* the other day, getting a new crown?

ERIC. Yeah…?

ZIMMER. There you are in *Time* magazine! *Time* magazine! Has a write-up on *my* friend Ricky Weiss! I couldn't believe it, I showed everybody there! The girl at the desk?, *every*body. "See this guy? We grew up together! In Sheepshead Bay! Like brothers, practically! Twins!" Oh, yeah, and in the thing?, in the write-up?, when they mention the friend in the book he gets bar mitzvahed with?

ERIC. Seth Bernstein.

ZIMMER. Seth Bernstein! Yeah! The friend he gets bar *mitzvahed* with? Wait a minute: That's *me!*

ERIC. Well … not *you*, exactly …

ZIMMER. *(Continuous.)* I had to have that book! I run home, get online, order the book — and I want you to know you should be honored: I *never* buy hard-covered books — *ever.* Ask Mindy; if it takes a *year*, I wait for paper. But *this* one; how could I wait? I'm *in* this book! Book comes, tear it open, start reading. Cannot. Put. It. Down. I mean, *hours* go by. Kids can't find me; Mindy can't find me: "*I-raaa!*" I'm in the john, reading! *(Eric chuckles. Half joking.)* Couldn't count on the *author* sending me an autographed *copy* or anything …

ERIC. Hey, if I knew where to send it …

ZIMMER. Same address. 1911 Avenue X.

ERIC. Your parents' house?

ZIMMER. Yup. House I grew up in. Now my kids are growing up in it.

ERIC. No kidding. With your mom?

ZIMMER. With my mom. Why, you think it's weird?

ERIC. No no …

ZIMMER. You think it's weird I sleep in my parents' old *bed*-room?

ERIC. *(Equivocally.)* No …

ZIMMER. Okay, maybe it *is* a little weird. The *bed* is new at least. Well, the mattress — So aren't you gonna ask me what I thought?

ERIC. What you thought…?

ZIMMER. Of *Brooklyn Boy*!

ERIC. I was just going to.

ZIMMER. I hated it. *(Off Eric's look; he cracks up.)* I'm only *kibitzing! Look* at you! I really had you going that time! Whataya *think* I thought?! I loved it!

ERIC. Oh, good!

ZIMMER. Are you kidding? How could I not love it? It's the story of my life! I mean, literally! The playgrounds and living rooms you write about, I *know* them! I was *there!* One or two things you got wrong but still …

ERIC. How could it be "wrong," it's fiction.

ZIMMER. Some of the real stuff was better. You should've called me, I could've helped you out. That's okay; it's still good. And that Seth Bernstein character! Obviously modeled on someone very brilliant.

ERIC. Seth Bernstein is not you.

ZIMMER. Yeah, right.

ERIC. He's not.

ZIMMER. Whataya talking about, "not me"? Of course he's me. He's got "me" written all over him!

ERIC. He's a composite of a lot of people I grew up with.

ZIMMER. Especially *me*. The acne on the back? The undescended testicle?!

ERIC. You had an undescended testicle?

ZIMMER. You *know* I did.

ERIC. I forgot about that.

ZIMMER. See? You don't even realize how *much* he's me.

ERIC. He's a fictional character.

ZIMMER. What, like Kenny Fleischman isn't you? Arnie Fleischman isn't your dad? Who you trying to kid?

ERIC. Ira …

ZIMMER. Why can't you just admit I inspired you? Huh? Why

25

can't you give me that much? I'm not gonna sue you or anything. I don't care how rich you get off of me, I just want to hear you say it. The guy is me! I even gave it to my *mother* to read!

ERIC. And?…

ZIMMER. *She* thought he was me. Definitely.

ERIC. What did she think of the *book*.

ZIMMER. *(Equivocally.)* She liked it.

ERIC. *(Picking up on his reservation.)* Yeah?…

ZIMMER. *You* know. She had some quibbles here and there.

ERIC. Like what?

ZIMMER. She thought it was anti-Semitic.

ERIC. *(Like a punch in the gut.)* Ooh, really?

ZIMMER. Not me, that's what *she* thought.

ERIC. Gee, I'm sorry to hear that.

ZIMMER. She didn't care for your depiction.

ERIC. My depiction?

ZIMMER. Of Brooklyn Jews. She didn't like it, she thought it was condescending.

ERIC. She said that? Your mother used the word "condescending"?

ZIMMER. No, that's *my* word.

ERIC. What did *she* say?

ZIMMER. I think she used the word "snotty."

ERIC. Uy. She didn't think it was funny?

ZIMMER. No. She hated what you did to your mother.

ERIC. The *protagonist's* mother.

ZIMMER. Whatever; *you* know: the main kid's mother. She thought it was mean. The pill-popping and stuff? The diet pills?

ERIC. Did *you* think it was funny?

ZIMMER. Me? Yeah! Are you kidding?

ERIC. But your mother failed to see the "aching ruefulness that underlies the comedy"? You see the reviews on the back?

ZIMMER. My mother doesn't know from "aching ruefulness."

ERIC. She just didn't like it.

ZIMMER. She didn't just not like it, she HATED it.

ERIC. *(Amused, sort of.)* Okay!

ZIMMER. Hey, while you're here, you should stop by and see her.

ERIC. Why? So she can yell at me?

ZIMMER. No! It would be a mitzvah. She would love to see you. You always meant so much to her.

ERIC. I did?

ZIMMER. Yes! She was crazy about you. Are you kidding? So she

26

didn't like your book. Big deal!

ERIC. She HATED my book.

ZIMMER. She's still proud of *you*. We're *all* proud of you! God, your dad! Your dad must be like…!

ERIC. Yeah. He is.

ZIMMER. If it was somebody else?, someone undeserving having this success? It would really piss me off. But *you*. Whatever good stuff comes your way, you deserve it.

ERIC. Thank you, Ira. I appreciate that.

ZIMMER. You really stuck *to* it. You didn't give up. And I really gotta hand it to you. 'Cause after those *other* books of yours … The *first* two … *(Shakes his head.)* Whatever the "message" or whatever, went *(Whistles.)* wayyy over my head.

ERIC. I know; they weren't for everybody. The *critics* liked them, though.

ZIMMER. *(Over " … though.")* I'm not talking critics now, I'm talking regular people — Is it okay for me to be saying this?

ERIC. *(With a laugh.)* Sure, what the hell.

ZIMMER. 'Cause I don't know what you're supposed to say to a writer.

ERIC. You can say whatever you like.

ZIMMER. I almost wrote you a letter.

ERIC. Yeah?

ZIMMER. Years ago. After your first book: *The Gentleman Farmer*.

ERIC. *(Impressed.)* Very good.

ZIMMER. I *told* you: I'm *up* on you. I *tried* reading it, I really did.

ERIC. It's okay.

ZIMMER. I read maybe fifty pages. *If* that. I didn't know where it was coming from. You know?

ERIC. It's really okay.

ZIMMER. *(Continuous.)* It didn't seem like *you* at all. It was like you were trying to be profound or something.

ERIC. *(Self-effacing.)* It was my first book!

ZIMMER. I kept thinking, where's Ricky in this? What's he writing this intellectual modern bullshit for? I was gonna write you and ask you point-blank. I wish I had. 'Cause, then — man! — that *second* book!

ERIC. *The Aerie*.

ZIMMER. Uy vey. Is *that* how you pronounce it?

ERIC. Uh-huh. It's a bird's nest.

ZIMMER. If someone put a gun to my head and said, "Tell me

what this book's about or I'll shoot," I'd be shot — dead — right on the spot.

ERIC. *(Making light of his discomfort.)* So, how are *you*, by the way?

ZIMMER. Who am *I* to tell *you*, right?

ERIC. *(Dismissively.)* No no no.

ZIMMER. *(Continuous.)* You're the published writer. Who am *I*. Just some schmuck who runs a deli.

ERIC. Is that really what you do?

ZIMMER. Why? You expected maybe something more exalted from me? I run my father's deli. Remember my dad and my uncle had a deli?

ERIC. Oh yeah, on, uh …

ZIMMER. Kings Highway, right near the station.

ERIC. Kings Highway. Right! So now it's yours?

ZIMMER. Yup. Mine, all mine.

ERIC. That's great.

ZIMMER. Come on.

ERIC. What.

ZIMMER. You don't think it's "great"; I certainly don't think it's "great." What's so great about it? My dad drops dead, my uncle sees it as a sign from God, *he* picks up, moves to Boca, my mom is a basket case, my *sis*ter doesn't want anything to do with the place, so who do you think the deli lands on, like a house fallin' outta the sky? *(A beat.)* Ya know? I used to *wish* him dead. I did; I *prayed* he would just go away and leave me the hell alone. Then whataya know? One day I show up to work after class? Ambulance, cops, people on the street. I think, sonofabitch. You're not supposed to get what you wish for, you know. Screws you up big time if you do.

ERIC. I'm sorry.

ZIMMER. It was only supposed to be for the time being. Who thinks forever when you're twenty-one, twenty-two? A *year* goes by, then *five* years, then before you know it, *you're* the *alter cocker* behind the counter flingin' the Hebrew Nationals. Some old customers come in, see me, and think I *am* my father! That he didn't die! That he and I are the same person! *(A beat.)* Need a story for your next book? Oh, I've got a story. Only I'm gonna *charge* you for it this time. *(Pause.)*

ERIC. Ira…? It was a pleasure running into you. *(Moves to go.)*

ZIMMER. Where you going?!

ERIC. I should head back to the city.

ZIMMER. That's it?! I don't see you for twenty-five years, that's all

28

I get?!

ERIC. I really should go.

ZIMMER. It's *shabbos.* Come home with me for *shabbos.*

ERIC. *(Over "… for shabbos.")* Oh, no, I couldn't —

ZIMMER. You gonna shlep all the way back to the city?

ERIC. My wife is expecting me; plus, I've got a flight early in the morning.

ZIMMER. Where you going?

ERIC. L.A.

ZIMMER. *L.A.?!* Really? You going Hollywood, Ricky? Huh? You sell your book to the movies?

ERIC. Actually, I did.

ZIMMER. You did? You DID?! *Mazel tov!*

ERIC. I guess.

ZIMMER. We should celebrate!

ERIC. *(Extends his hand in a gesture of farewell.)* Ira…?

ZIMMER. *(Urgently.)* I got a million things I want to say to you! You know how many times I'd see some guy on the subway, walking, in the city — and swear it was you?

ERIC. Really.

ZIMMER. He'd come closer and my heart would beat faster and faster, so excited I was finally gonna get to *talk* to you again, then the guy would go by … and he'd look nothing like you.

ERIC. Ira, I wish you all the best.

ZIMMER. I can't believe you're doing this to me again.

ERIC. Doing what?

ZIMMER. *(Continuous.)* I try to get close to you and you push me away.

ERIC. I'm not pushing you away; I have to go.

ZIMMER. Did I do something to you?

ERIC. What?

ZIMMER. Something that made you stop wanting to be friends with me?

ERIC. No! You didn't do anything. We grew up, that's all.

ZIMMER. Everybody grows up.

ERIC. People outgrow each other.

ZIMMER. I didn't outgrow *you.*

ERIC. Ira …

ZIMMER. How come I didn't outgrow *you?* Huh? I always loved you.

ERIC. Oh, God …

ZIMMER. I did. Should I not have said that?

ERIC. No.

ZIMMER. You think that makes me queer or something?

ERIC. No, of course not.

ZIMMER. I loved you. Even when you decided I wasn't cool enough for you anymore.

ERIC. Ira …

ZIMMER. You needed to impress your *goyishe* new Ivy League friends.

ERIC. That is ridiculous.

ZIMMER. The minute I heard you got into Columbia, I knew that was it.

ERIC. That was what?

ZIMMER. You were gone, you were outta here, and never coming back. I *called* you, left *messages* for you … You never had time for me!

ERIC. I was busy with school!

ZIMMER. So was I! But you were always so "vital." No matter what *I* was doing, what *you* were doing was way more important. I was busy, too! Maybe it was *only* Brooklyn College, it wasn't Columbia …

ERIC. You could've tried for a place like Columbia!

ZIMMER. No I couldn't've! There was *no way* my parents could afford it!

ERIC. What, you think *my* parents were rich? What is this fantasy you have of me? *You* were in that shoe store; you saw that apartment. They never had any money — I worked my ass off to get a scholarship! Otherwise I never would've gotten the hell out of here!

ZIMMER. See, it never even *occurred* to me that I could do that! I thought that was for other people. I was smart! I had potential! Nobody ever pulled me aside and told me it was okay to go for it! Nobody! Nobody ever told me I could aspire to *any*thing!

ERIC. Nobody ever told *me*, either! I figured it out for myself.

ZIMMER. How? How'd you do it? What is it, a gene? A chemical? What is it you were born with that I wasn't? We were born three days apart!

ERIC. I know.

ZIMMER. Right here, right in this very hospital! Lived three blocks away. Saw each other every day, practically. Now look where *you* are and look where *I* am.

ERIC. Where am I? I'm in a hospital cafeteria in Brooklyn — just like you — with a parent upstairs who's dying. *(Pause.)* Goodbye,

Ira. Good luck with everything.

ZIMMER. Hey, they got a nice little *shul* here, right in the lobby; I'm gonna *dahven* before I go home. Why don't you come *with* me.

ERIC. No, no, go. Do what you have to do.

ZIMMER. It's right here; right down the hall.

ERIC. *(Over " ... right down ... ")* No, thanks. Now I really have to go.

ZIMMER. Ten minutes. We'll say a little *brucha* for my mom and your dad.

ERIC. No.

ZIMMER. What, you're a Rosh Hashanah Jew now, Ricky? Huh? You fast on Yom Kippur, that's it for the year?

ERIC. Actually, I don't fast; I don't do anything.

ZIMMER. *(Over " ... I don't do anything.")* No? You don't?

ERIC. The last time I was in temple was the day of our bar mitzvah.

ZIMMER. Well, we'll see about *that* ... *(Takes Eric's arm.)* Come. Let's get you back into the fold!

ERIC. *(Pulls away brusquely; too harshly.)* NO! *(Zimmer, taken aback, puts his hands up. Pause.)* Look, Ira, I wish you all the best. I really do.

ZIMMER. Uh-huh.

ERIC. *(Starts to go.)* Take care.

ZIMMER. Have fun in Hollywood.

ERIC. Yeah, thanks.

ZIMMER. See ya. *(Eric waves, goes. A beat. Calls.)* Hey! Who's gonna play me in the movie?!

Scene 3

St. Mark's Place

That night. An apartment in the East Village. Eric has entered carrying a shopping bag; Nina is there. A pile of galleys is on the table and a box stuffed with books, CDs, LPs, is nearby.

NINA. What's the matter, you don't believe in doorbells?

ERIC. Sorry. Force of habit. *(He pockets his keys, tries to kiss her but is rebuffed.)*

NINA. What happened? You said six.

ERIC. *Around* six.

NINA. 6:40 is not around six; 6:40 is almost seven.

ERIC. I'm sorry. I stopped off at Szechuan Garden.

NINA. Why?

ERIC. To get us some food.

NINA. Who said anything about food?

ERIC. *(Coming further into the room.)* You rearranged.

NINA. Rick? Who said anything about *food?*

ERIC. *(Over " … about food?")* How come *we* never thought to put the table here? Looks good. *(Unpacks take-out containers.)*

NINA. *(Over "Looks good.")* What are you doing?

ERIC. Sautéed string beans …

NINA. Rick …

ERIC. Steamed dumplings …

NINA. What are you *do*ing?

ERIC. *(Bad accent.)* I bring you a feast.

NINA. I don't want a feast.

ERIC. Mmm … The dumplings look especially succulent this evening.

NINA. This may come as a shock to you but this is not a date. Do you realize that?

ERIC. It's beginning to dawn on me, yeah.

NINA. If anything, it's the *opposite* of a date.

ERIC. An anti-date. Hey. Aren't you hungry? I'm starving; I haven't eaten anything all day.

NINA. This is classic! It's the story of our marriage: *You* were hungry, so we're eating!

ERIC. It was purely spontaneous; there was nothing diabolical about it.

NINA. How do you know I haven't already eaten?

ERIC. Have you?

NINA. That's not the point. How do you know I don't have dinner plans?

ERIC. Do you?

NINA. That's not the *point!* Everything is always *you*, always what *you* want.

ERIC. *(Innocently.)* Are you seeing someone?

NINA. *(More incredulous than angry.)* None of your fucking business!

ERIC. *(Hands up in surrender.)* Okay!

NINA. Look, why don't you just take your shit and go. *(Meaning the box.)*

ERIC. *(Winces.)* Is that nice?

NINA. It's my fault: I never should've said it was okay to stop by, I should've just *mailed* it.

ERIC. Neen … come on …

NINA. And I think you'd better give me your key.

ERIC. Why?!

NINA. I can't have you waltzing in here like this …

ERIC. *(Over " … like this … ")* Come on … Can we please call a truce? I thought we were going to try "civil" for a change. Can we do that? Can we at least try? *(Long pause. Her anger abates; she shows him a stack of mail.)*

NINA. All this is yours, you know. *(He nods.)* I thought you said you sent in your change-of-address card.

ERIC. I did. I can't help it if things fall through the cracks.

NINA. *(Hefts the mail.)* Those are *some* cracks. *(A beat. She flips through the mail.)* Your mail's certainly gotten more interesting lately. It *feels* weightier. Books to review, invitations. All *I* get are bills. Bills and rejection letters. So, you were on the *Today* show?

ERIC. Did you see it?

NINA. No. The guy downstairs with the plucked eyebrows told me. He was thrilled.

ERIC. Good. I'm glad the guy with the plucked eyebrows was thrilled. *(A beat.)* How've you been?

NINA. I've been great.

ERIC. You *look* great.

NINA. I *feel* great.

ERIC. It actually hurts my pride a little how great you look.

NINA. Why? I'm not supposed to look great?

ERIC. No; you were supposed to languish, and look like shit. Like me.

NINA. Why are you languishing?

ERIC. Haven't you heard? My wife is divorcing me. *(He offers a dumpling; she waves off his offer. Pause.)*

NINA. How was Brooklyn?

ERIC. Depressing.

NINA. The borough or your father?

ERIC. Both.

NINA. How is he?

ERIC. Not good.

NINA. I'm sorry to hear that.

ERIC. *(Over " … to hear that.")* He says this is it this time.

NINA. Oh, he's been saying that for years.

ERIC. Yeah but it has a distinctly different ring to it this time.

NINA. Poor Manny. I really have to call him.

ERIC. That would be great.

NINA. *(Nods, a beat.)* How'd he take it?

ERIC. *(Sheepishly.)* Well … I didn't actually …

NINA. Rick! …

ERIC. I'm sorry, I couldn't do it.

NINA. *(Over " … do it.")* You said you were finally going to tell him!

ERIC. *(Over " … tell him!")* I know.

NINA. What are you waiting for? You're running out of time.

ERIC. I didn't see the point of giving him bad news.

NINA. He's your father, he deserves to know what's going on in your life.

ERIC. *(Over " … in your life.")* Yeah but what's he supposed to *do* with information like this? *(A beat.)* He asks about you all the time.

NINA. And what do you tell him?

ERIC. I tell him you're busy. *(She shakes her head.)* *Call* him, he would love to hear from you.

NINA. And what am I supposed to do? Keep up the pretense that we're still together?

ERIC. Is that really too much to ask?

NINA. It's a lie. You're asking me to lie.

ERIC. *(Over " … to lie.")* I'm asking you to spare him one more blow. The man has no future, nothing to look forward to … Christ, he's still holding out for a grandchild! *(Silence. Refers to voluminous galleys.)* What's this?

NINA. *(Takes the pile.)* Nothing, just some bullshit computer science text I'm proofing.

ERIC. Are you writing?

NINA. *(Defensively.)* Yes I'm writing. That's what I do: I write.

ERIC. *(Wearily.)* I know that's what you do. How's it going?

NINA. It's going. I don't write autobiographically, you know, so I don't have a bottomless well to draw from.

ERIC. Ah, yes …

NINA. *(Continuous.)* *My* writing requires a bit more invention. A bit more imagination.

ERIC. *(Over " … imagination.")* That's right, writing autobiographically isn't really writing.

NINA. What about you? What are *you* working on?

ERIC. Nothing.

NINA. Why?

ERIC. No time. This goddamn tour.

NINA. *Where* were you this week, Florida? *(He nods.)* How was it?

ERIC. Well, imagine my Aunt Rose, replicated thousands of times over.

NINA. *(Laughs.)* Oh, God …

ERIC. Uy, and the so-called "talks" at Jewish centers where all the *alter cockers* do all the talking! *(She laughs.)* These are My People, apparently: ancient, displaced, Brooklyn Jews, all of them deaf.

NINA. *(Laughs, then.)* You don't have to do this, you know. You *could* just say no.

ERIC. And forfeit my fifteen minutes? Are you kidding? I waited all my life to be this miserable. *(She laughs. Pause.)* It's a bestseller, by the way.

NINA. It is? *(He nods.)* Really?

ERIC. It's official. This Sunday: I'm on The List.

NINA. *(Moved to tears.)* Oh, Rick, that's wonderful. Congratulations.

ERIC. *(Over "Congratulations.")* Thanks … Thank you.

NINA. You made it.

ERIC. Yeah. I guess.

NINA. God, look at me … *(He touches her; she composes herself.)* What number?

ERIC. Eleven.

NINA. Respectable.

ERIC. Or as my father said, "You mean there *is* an eleven?"

NINA. How'd you find out?

ERIC. Marian called, shouting into the phone — I was in the rec room of a condo development in Sunrise, Florida. It was surreal. I got off and instinctively called *you.*

NINA. You did?

ERIC. *(Shakes his head.)* I stopped. Thought I'd better get used to not having you to talk to. *(Silence.)* What are we doing?

NINA. Rick.

ERIC. I *miss* you. I can't *sleep* without you.

NINA. *(Over "I can't … ")* Oh, God …

ERIC. Okay, so we tried separation …

NINA. Please don't start.

ERIC. *(Continuous.)* We gave it a couple of months; it isn't working.

NINA. For *you* maybe.

ERIC. This is The Good Part! You're bailing out on The Good Part?! We can finally live like grown-ups!

NINA. Rick …

ERIC. *(Continuous.)* We've never been "us" with money before. Don't you want to see what that's like?

NINA. Go home.

ERIC. What are you doing tomorrow?

NINA. Why?

ERIC. I fly to L.A. in the morning. Why don't you come with me?

NINA. Why would I do that?

ERIC. So we can talk.

NINA. What is *this*? *(Meaning this conversation.)*

ERIC. I mean really talk.

NINA. Six hours in an airplane talking about our relationship, I'd rather die.

ERIC. We'll hang out for a few days. They're putting me up in one of those ridiculous hotels. It'll be fun.

NINA. Shlepping along on your book tour is not my idea of fun.

ERIC. Why must you see it as shlepping along?

NINA. You know how it is: I become totally irrelevant.

ERIC. No you don't.

NINA. *(Over " … you don't.")* It happened with *The Aerie!* And that was nothing compared to this.

ERIC. It won't be like that, I promise.

NINA. *(Over " … I promise.")* Of course it'll be like that. You have no idea what it's like having to stand there, smiling like an idiot, hoping *someone* makes eye contact with you. It's demoralizing.

ERIC. *(Over "It's demoralizing.")* I always make a point of introducing you to everyone! I tell everybody what a wonderful writer you are!

NINA. Yes and I *hate* it when you do that! It makes me feel like a fucking charity case when you do that!

ERIC. I'm sorry! Jesus!

NINA. Everyone knows I haven't had a story published in six years. Who do you think you're fooling?

ERIC. *(Over "Who do … ")* Nobody cares. That's all in your head.

NINA. All in my head? Come on, *six years?* And it hasn't occurred to you I might not be any good? *(He doesn't respond. Pause.)* I wish I could've been a different sort of partner for you, Rick, I really do.

ERIC. *(Over " … I really do.")* What are you talking about?

NINA. You'd've been much better off with an adoring little wifeytype.

ERIC. No I wouldn't have.

NINA. *(Continuous.)* But that's not who I am. I'm way too selfish and competitive.

ERIC. Yes and that's what I've always loved about you.

NINA. I don't know how you put up with me as long as you did. The contagion of failure should've been overwhelming. Between the miscarriages and the rejection letters …

ERIC. We can look into adoption again.

NINA. No no no. You still don't get it.

ERIC. *(Over "You still … ")* We can really afford it now.

NINA. I don't want a baby. I *wanted* a baby. *Our* baby. I'm over it. My maternal instinct is dead. I've done all the mourning I can possibly do. Now I want my life back. *(Pause.)* We let that farce go on way too long. Infertility was my full-time job. What the hell, I needed a *real* job, anyway, right, Rick?

ERIC. We were trying to conceive.

NINA. *(Vulnerably.)* Why didn't you say it was okay to stop?!

ERIC. What?

NINA. You never said it. That's all I needed to hear.

ERIC. Sweetie … *(He holds her.)*

NINA. *(Notices the time.)* Oh, shit, you've really got to go now.

ERIC. Wait.

NINA. Please, Rick. I have someone coming.

ERIC. *(A beat; wounded.)* Oh.

NINA. I'm sorry. I know this is awkward; I didn't want this to happen.

ERIC. Uh-huh. *(Starts cleaning up.)*

NINA. You were forty minutes late; if you were here when you *said* you were going to be here.

ERIC. *(Over " … you were going to … ")* You're right; no, you're absolutely right.

NINA. I'm sorry. *(Meaning the food.)* Leave it; I'll do it.

ERIC. Save it. There's plenty for lunch.

NINA. Well then *you* take it.

ERIC. No no, you, I won't get to eat it; I'll be in L.A.

NINA. Oh, right. Okay. Thanks. *(He bends to lift the box.)* Carry it from the bottom, it's pretty heavy.

ERIC. *(Over " … it's pretty heavy"; amused by the weight.)* Jesus, what the hell have you *got* in here?

NINA. I decided you can have the Elvis Costellos.

ERIC. Really? *(She nods.)* Your loss. *(He opens the box and removes a pair of sandals.)*

NINA. I wasn't sure what you wanted to do with those.

ERIC. They're shot. We can toss 'em. *(He takes a book from the box.)*

NINA. Did you know you left your *Magic Mountain*?

ERIC. No, I took the new translation.

NINA. Oh. Well, *I* don't want this edition.

ERIC. So give it away.

NINA. *You* give it away.

ERIC. All right …

NINA. No, I'll do it; I've got stuff going to the thrift shop anyway. *(Perplexed, he pulls out an old cable-knit sweater.)*

ERIC. This is yours.

NINA. It *was* yours. You got it in Maine.

ERIC. Yeah, I remember, but I gave it to *you*.

NINA. I know, but I thought you might like to have it back.

ERIC. Come on, you loved this sweater.

NINA. I know I did. But I can't see myself wearing it anymore, and I know you were always fond of it, so …

ERIC. Do you *hate* me?

NINA. What? No. It's just … Whenever I see you, or smell your scent on an old sweater, I'm reminded of all the things I failed at. And I can't live like that anymore. *(A beat.)* Goodbye, Ricky. Congratulations. *(He looks bemused.)* Number eleven.

ERIC. Oh, yeah. Neen, I wish you would just — *(She kisses him on the mouth.)*

NINA. Save it for your next novel. *(Remembers.)* Oh — your key. *(Grudgingly, he takes his key ring out of his pocket and removes the key.)*

ERIC. So this is it? This is the end?

NINA. This is it, bubbie. It's over. This is what the end looks like. *(She holds out her hand. He gives her his key.)*

End of Act One

ACT TWO

Scene 4

Mondrian

Night. A suite in the Mondrian Hotel. In subdued light we find Eric looking out the window at the twinkling amber lights of West Hollywood. Off, a toilet flushes. Alison emerges from the adjoining (unseen) sitting area.

ALISON. Cool bathroom. *(A beat.)* You mind if I check out the minibar?

ERIC. Go right ahead. *(She ducks out again. A beat. Calls:)* Can you grab me a water?

ALISON. *(Off.)* Sure. *(Returns balancing bottles of water and snacks, and drops her loot on the bed.)*

ERIC. *(Amused.)* What *is* all that?

ALISON. Too much? I'm sorry, I can put some back.

ERIC. *(Over " … I can … ")* No no, it's okay. If you're *that* hungry, we can always order room service.

ALISON. No, this is fine; this is perfect. I eat like this all the time. Want to split a KitKat?

ERIC. Sure, I'll help you out with that. *(She gives him half.)* Given minibar inflation, this is probably a ten-dollar KitKat.

ALISON. *(Wince.)* Oooh, you're right.

ERIC. Don't worry about it. It's on Paramount.

ALISON. Paramount as in Paramount Pictures?

ERIC. You don't think *publishers* put writers up in hotels like this.

ALISON. I have no idea.

ERIC. No, leave it to the movies to know the meaning of excess. I'm here on Paramount's dime. They optioned my book.

ALISON. Oh!

ERIC. I wrote the screenplay.

ALISON. Oh, wow!

ERIC. We'll see how "oh, wow." I'm getting "notes" from my producer in the morning.

ALISON. That is so cool. *(Pause.)*

ERIC. Pass the M&M's? *(She does.)*

ALISON. There's this movie I wrote I want to produce independently?

ERIC. Oh, yeah? What is it?

ALISON. It's set in the future? On a space colony?

ERIC. Uh-huh.

ALISON. Where the first generation of children born there — do you really want to hear this?

ERIC. Yeah. Absolutely.

ALISON. Okay, so these kids were all conceived like right around the same time and now they're like sixteen, seventeen years old going through all the usual rebellious earthling shit teenagers go through — sex and drugs and stuff?

ERIC. Uh-huh.

ALISON. Only they spent their whole lives on this like weird, hermetic colony in the middle of outer space, but it's the only home they've ever known, okay?

ERIC. Yeah? …

ALISON. And now this like utopian society is on the brink of like total ecological disaster. So, in order to save the colony, they band together to overthrow their leaders — *who also happen to be their parents.*

ERIC. They overthrow them?

ALISON. Uh-huh.

ERIC. How?

ALISON. They, *you* know, they *kill* them.

ERIC. They kill their parents?

ALISON. Yeah, one by one, in really cool ways.

ERIC. Huh.

ALISON. So, like, in the third act, all the grown-ups are dead, okay?

ERIC. Yeah? …

ALISON. And there they are, the kids, the new generation, finally in control, right? — in the middle of all this carnage — there are like body parts everywhere, it's really gross.

ERIC. Uch.

ALISON. And you know what they discover?

ERIC. What.

ALISON. They're *still* doomed! They're just as clueless as their parents! *(A beat.)* And that's my movie.

ERIC. Hm.

ALISON. People say it's awesome. It's an allegory.

ERIC. It's interesting, it really is. So, let me ask you, when you come up with a story like that, how do you know it's a screenplay?

ALISON. What do you mean?

ERIC. What makes it a movie and not a novel?

ALISON. It's a movie. It *has* to be a movie.

ERIC. Yeah, I know, but what if you actually wrote the story as a piece of fiction.

ALISON. Why? That would be like such a waste of time. No offense or anything, but fiction is like *so* over.

ERIC. *(Amused.)* Really.

ALISON. I mean, don't get me wrong, I *love* books. And I really respect people like you who still bother to write them.

ERIC. It seems almost "quaint" to you, huh?

ALISON. Like watchmakers or violin-makers or something. People who devote themselves so completely to a dying craft? It's touching, it really is.

ERIC. You know, if I let myself think like that, I'd have a pretty hard time getting up in the morning.

ALISON. I don't know how you do it. I really don't. It takes a lot of courage to do what you do. Who do you do it for?

ERIC. What do you mean "who"?

ALISON. I mean, besides yourself. Who's your audience?

ERIC. Uh …

ALISON. Middle-aged or old people who have the time and the money to buy books and read them? That's nothing; that's like a tiny, miniscule fraction of the population. Kids *my* age don't read. They don't. I mean, it's not that they're illiterate, it's just that it's not an important part of their lives. The only stories *they* like are the kind that can be *shown* to them. All they have to do is sit there and let it wash over them. I mean, why read when they could much more easily go to a movie or rent a DVD or something? Why spend like thirty bucks on a book that might not even be any good 'cause even books that are *supposed* to be good are rarely as good as they say they are, they're just hyped to get you to buy them.

ERIC. *(Teasing.)* You are being way harsh.

ALISON. I'm sorry.

ERIC. Why'd you come hear me read tonight if this is how you feel?

ALISON. I'm not saying this is how *I* feel, I'm saying this is how kids my *age* feel. I wanted to meet you. I'd read *The Aerie* and I —

ERIC. You *did? (She nods.)* When?

ALISON. A long time ago. Like three years ago.

ERIC. *That* long ago?

ALISON. *(Swats at him, then.)* You know how you read a book and you want to meet the author? If you *do* meet them … you pray to God they don't turn out to be a schmuck or something?

ERIC. How'm I doing?

ALISON. You're doing okay. I liked your voice when you read tonight, at Book Soup.

ERIC. Oh, yeah? Thanks. So you liked *The Aerie*?

ALISON. Yeah, it's like one of my all-time favorites. First time I read it, I couldn't stop crying.

ERIC. Really?

ALISON. When the nest is destroyed by the storm? God. It was so beautiful. Every sentence. It was like poetry, the whole book, it really was.

ERIC. Thank you. It's being reissued in paperback.

ALISON. Wow, that is really great!

ERIC. Yeah, that and *The Gentleman Farmer*. Out of print for years, now they can't be rushed back into print fast enough.

ALISON. That is so cool.

ERIC. See? If you live long enough, anything'll happen. *(They smile at one another. Pause.)*

ALISON. What do people call you?

ERIC. What?

ALISON. Your friends. What do they call you?

ERIC. *(Shrugs.)* Eric.

ALISON. Just Eric?

ERIC. Rick. Ricky.

ALISON. *(Delighted.)* Ricky?!

ERIC. People who've known me a long time call me Ricky.

ALISON. I love it! I'm gonna call you Ricky!

ERIC. *(Sharper than intended.)* No you're not.

ALISON. *(Embarrassed.)* Sorry.

ERIC. *(Easing the sting.)* Ricky's reserved for a select few. A rapidly *diminishing* few. *(A beat.)* Why my mother and father named a Jewish boy "Eric" … As far as I could tell, there *is* no Eric in the Old Testament. *(She laughs.)* I looked. When I was about eight or nine I discovered I had the same name as Houdini, and suddenly it was cool to be an Eric.

ALISON. I know I should know who that is.

42

ERIC. Harry Houdini. The Great Houdini.

ALISON. Was he like a famous magician or something?

ERIC. Illusionist. Escape artist of legend.

ALISON. Oh, yeah.

ERIC. His given name was Erich Weiss. Erich with an "H" at the end.

ALISON. You were named after him?

ERIC. No, it was a coincidence; my parents didn't know that was his real name. I remember my grandfather telling me stories about the Great Houdini.

ALISON. Oh, yeah?

ERIC. He saw him once, back in the twenties, on the Lower East Side. Houdini had these heavy chains wrapped around him and they locked him inside a steamer trunk. Then the trunk was thrown off a pier into the East River.

ALISON. Wow.

ERIC. It was wintertime; it was freezing. The crowd waited for him to come up — minutes went by; they were certain he'd frozen to death — when, finally, miraculously, he *burst* to the surface and everybody cheered!

ALISON. Wow!

ERIC. I've come to see that Houdini and I actually have more in common than our names. We're both escape artists.

ALISON. What did *you* ever escape from?

ERIC. *(Matter-of-factly.)* Brooklyn. *(They share a smile.)*

ALISON. Speaking of which … *(Gets* Brooklyn Boy *out of her bag.)*

ERIC. Uh-oh.

ALISON. Oh no it is so good.

ERIC. What are you up to? *(Meaning, in the book.)*

ALISON. I just started; I read like the first few pages in the bookstore. The leftie day camp?

ERIC. Camp Zion.

ALISON. Yeah. Kenny changing into his bathing suit?

ERIC. Uh-huh.

ALISON. Oh, God, it's so awful.

ERIC. Awful?

ALISON. So awful, it's hysterical. Everyone's worst humiliation nightmare. Did that really happen like that, the girls walking by and laughing and stuff?

ERIC. Why?

ALISON. You can't make something like that up; it's too horrible. It *has* to be true.

ERIC. Why is that so important?

ALISON. What.

ERIC. Knowing that something is true. People are always asking me, "Is that you, did that really happen?" As if that has any bearing on anything. What is that about? *(She gets cigarettes from her bag and smokes.)*

ALISON. You're Kenny, right?

ERIC. That's what I mean!

ALISON. It's no secret, right? Kenny is you.

ERIC. Not me. A *version* of me. A "me" I might have been.

ALISON. Were you really such a dorky kid?

ERIC. He isn't "dorky."

ALISON. He's pretty dorky.

ERIC. He is not. Kenny's an Everyboy. Kenny Fleischman is anyone who's ever felt like an outsider.

ALISON. Sounds like a copy line you'd see in an ad or something.

ERIC. Sorry; I've been giving too many interviews lately. *(She laughs; he smiles. Pause.)* You really shouldn't smoke, you know.

ALISON. Yeah and *you* shouldn't take girls half your age back to hotel rooms.

ERIC. *(A wince.)* Oooh.

ALISON. Gummy bear?

ERIC. No thanks. You know, I never quite understood the appeal of gummy bears.

ALISON. Really? Oh, they're wonderful.

ERIC. What's so wonderful about them? They always get stuck in your teeth.

ALISON. I don't know, they're so small and smooth and translucent? *(Shows her palm.)* See? They're like little nuggets of sea glass or something. *(They look at one another. A sexually charged moment, which she defuses.)* So — don't you have like a *wife* or something?

ERIC. Is that what you want to talk about? My wife?

ALISON. *(Over "My wife?")* No, it's just I remember the bio thing with your picture on the cover of *The Aerie*, said you had a wife.

ERIC. That's true, it did.

ALISON. And on this one, it's like, wait a minute, where's the wife?

ERIC. Very astute detective work.

ALISON. Oh God, she didn't *die* or anything?

ERIC. No no, she didn't die. She just doesn't want to be married to me anymore, that's all.

ALISON. *(Over " ... that's all.")* Really? Why? What did you do?

44

ERIC. What do you *mean* what did I do? Why do you assume it was something *I* did?

ALISON. Happens all the time: Middle-aged man gets famous, goes completely sex-crazed, fucks up his marriage.

ERIC. I see you've done research on this.

ALISON. It's exactly what happened with my dad. He's not a famous writer or anything, he just made a lot of money out here.

ERIC. In the movie business?

ALISON. No, in plastic surgery. I mean, here's this average, shlumpy guy, and all of a sudden, like in his forties, he's this millionaire plastic surgeon and there are like all these *women* around, treating him like he's God or something and it's like he thinks he's been given this *imperative* to screw as many of them as possible. Never mind that my mother married him before he had *any*thing and put him through medical school and had his *chil*dren and everything. It's disgusting. *(A beat.)* So you're divorced?

ERIC. Not yet.

ALISON. But you're getting? *(He nods.)* Too bad.

ERIC. Yeah, it is.

ALISON. How many kids have you got?

ERIC. None.

ALISON. Well, *that's* good. Divorce and kids: Believe me, that sucks. So is she gonna fleece you now that you're famous?

ERIC. I don't know; I don't think she would do that.

ALISON. That's what my dad thought. My mom skinned him alive. *(A beat.)* So what went wrong? You mind my asking?

ERIC. Uh, well … It's complicated.

ALISON. How long were you together?

ERIC. Since graduate school.

ALISON. Wow. How come no kids? *(He shrugs, looks away. She understands.)* Oh.

ERIC. We met in Iowa. Nina and I. At the Writer's Workshop.

ALISON. She's a writer, too? *(He nods.)* Would I have ever heard of her?

ERIC. *(A beat.)* No. *(A beat.)* So, UCLA, right? *(She nods.)* Tell me again, *when* do you graduate?

ALISON. Next June. Soon I'll be one more overeducated assistant ordering Chinese chicken salad for some asshole producer.

ERIC. What do you *want* to do?

ALISON. I want to be the asshole producer.

ERIC. You don't want to write screenplays like everybody else out here?

ALISON. Nah. I wrote my movie; I got it out of my system. Sophomore year? I took screenwriting with this guy who makes all this money doctoring movies but never gets his name on anything?

ERIC. Uh-huh.

ALISON. See, I don't get that. No amount of money would make me give up having my name on something. I want my name right Out There, you know?, so people *know* me, know who I am. Otherwise why bother? You live a while and then you die.

ERIC. You want that badly to be famous?

ALISON. Yeah. Doesn't everybody? Look at *you*. Why did *you* want it?

ERIC. *(Shrugs; pause.)* My father sold shoes. In a Buster Brown store on Sheepshead Bay Road.

ALISON. He owned a shoe store?

ERIC. No, he worked for the man who did. He wasn't a partner, he was an employee. For thirty-nine years. He gave his life to that store. It wasn't even his to profit from, yet still he gave everything to that goddamn store. I could never understand what was so attractive about that place, why he chose to spend so much of his days there and not at home. *(A beat.)* I remember watching him closely in the morning, trying to uncover the mystery of manhood, the rituals of work. The shpritz of Aramis, the buff of the Oxfords, the tying of the perfect Windsor knot. I'd watch him from my window get swallowed up in the sea of Brooklyn fathers all beginning their day. *(He's moved.)* I should get you home.

ALISON. What? Oh. Okay? *(Pause.)* Is that it?

ERIC. What.

ALISON. Did I do something…?

ERIC. No.

ALISON. What happened? Can we start again? Please? I'll do whatever you want.

ERIC. Sweetie, it's okay.

ALISON. You sure I didn't do something?

ERIC. It's nothing you did. It's me.

ALISON. Did I talk too much?

ERIC. No!

ALISON. *(Continuous.)* Shit! I do that; I talk too much. I never know when to shut up.

ERIC. *(Over "I never … ")* It's all right. I've enjoyed talking to you.

ALISON. You just wanted to talk?

ERIC. I honestly don't know. *(Pause.)* Let me call for my car.
ALISON. Why?
ERIC. You left your car at Book Soup.
ALISON. It's not that far.
ERIC. What are you going to do, *walk?*
ALISON. Yeah, it's really not that far; just a few blocks.
ERIC. You're not walking down Sunset at two o'clock in the morning.
ALISON. " ... young lady." What are you, my *dad? (Pause.)* I don't *do* this, by the way.
ERIC. Do what.
ALISON. Go back to hotel rooms with famous older men and mooch off their minibars. I don't want you to think I'm a literary groupie or anything.
ERIC. I don't.
ALISON. Because that is so not who I am. You're my first famous writer. You're my first famous *any*thing.
ERIC. I'm flattered. I really am.
ALISON. You know? I'll bet you're one of those men who's better looking now than you've ever been in your entire life.
ERIC. What?
ALISON. I'll bet you are. And now that you're famous you have this power you never had before. Right? This *allure.* So it's Payback Time — right?
ERIC. What do you mean?
ALISON. All the girls in high school who never looked twice at you, there's like a whole new generation of them now, showing up at book signings, practically *throw*ing themselves at you. Right? I'll bet you played out *this* little scene in hotel rooms all across America.
ERIC. What little scene?
ALISON. This. Girl in Room.
ERIC. Is that what you think? I've been chalking up conquests, like a rock star on tour?
ALISON. Hey. I don't blame you. It's like everybody's revenge fantasy come true. Go for it.
ERIC. So if you thought I was so cynical, why'd you come back here with me?
ALISON. Why? You're Eric Weiss! What was I supposed to do? Tell you to fuck off?
ERIC. You certainly could've ...
ALISON. No way. Are you kidding? You chose *me.* You could've

47

left with like any one of six women and you picked *me!*

ERIC. *(Picks up the phone.)* Let me call for a cab.

ALISON. A *cab* to go to my *car?*

ERIC. *(Into phone.)* Yes, this is Eric Weiss in 806? Could you call for a cab for my friend?

ALISON. Your "friend"?

ERIC. *(Into phone.)* Thank you. *(Hangs up; gets cash from his wallet.)*

ALISON. What's that?

ERIC. Cab fare.

ALISON. What am I, a hooker? I can pay for my own taxi, thank you.

ERIC. I'm sorry.

ALISON. Look. Maybe you think you *owe* me something; you don't owe me *any*thing. I knew what I was doing coming here, okay? I knew when I left I'd have a story I'd tell the rest of my life. Everybody has one of those. This — tonight — is mine. *(The phone rings.)*

ERIC. *(Answers phone.)* Yes? Thank you. *(Hangs up.)* Your taxi's downstairs.

ALISON. Can I ask you something?

ERIC. Okay.

ALISON. This is gonna sound really lame under the circumstances ...

ERIC. What.

ALISON. *(A beat.)* Would you sign my book?

ERIC. Oh. Sure.

ALISON. *(Hands him the book.)* It's Alison, by the way.

ERIC. *(A lie.)* I know. One "L" or two?

ALISON. One. *(He inscribes her book, then hands it to her.)*

ERIC. There you go.

ALISON. *(Reads the inscription, then.)* Thanks.

ERIC. My pleasure. *(She goes.)*

Scene 5

Paramount

The following day. A producer's office on the Paramount lot. Desk, furniture with Santa Fe-style upholstery, foreign movie poster. Eric is seated. Melanie Fine, a movie producer, is talking on the phone.

MELANIE. *(Into her phone.)* Yeah, well, tell him *he's* not the one producing this movie, *I* am. And hold my calls — I want to give Mr. Weiss here my undivided attention. *(Winks at Eric.)* If *Jerry* calls, put him through. *(Stage whisper.)* Oh, and Caitlin? If you know who shows up, send him right in. *(Puts down the phone. To Eric.)* You okay with that? *(Meaning a bottle of water.)*
ERIC. Oh, yeah, I'm fine.
MELANIE. You sure you don't want a salad or a sandwich or something?
ERIC. No, no, this is fine.
MELANIE. Caitlin could get you something from the commissary.
ERIC. *(Over "… from the commissary.")* No, thanks. *(She responds to the message on her computer.)*
MELANIE. Onnne second … I'm allll yours … *(Finishes typing while he looks around and sips his water.)* So! How'd it go last night?!
ERIC. What.
MELANIE. Your book signing!
ERIC. Oh! Yeah!
MELANIE. *(Over "Yeah!")* Didn't you have your thing at Book Soup last night?
ERIC. *(Over "… last night?")* Yes. It went well.
MELANIE. I want to hear all about it. Nice turnout?
ERIC. Very nice; place was packed.
MELANIE. God, I'm so sorry I missed it!
ERIC. That's really okay. You know the book; you didn't need to hear me read.
MELANIE. I wanted to! It would've been fascinating! I love hearing writers read! Things got so crazy here; I've got a movie starts

49

shooting on the fifteenth, the script came in and was *such* a piece of shit, we were like frantic. Hey, congratulations!

ERIC. For what?

MELANIE. The bestseller list!

ERIC. Oh, yeah!

MELANIE. That is so fabulous!

ERIC. Thank you!

MELANIE. *Now* when we say "national bestseller" it'll actually be true! *(They laugh.)* Listen … I have the most incredible news.

ERIC. What.

MELANIE. I'm so glad you're out here so I can tell you in person!

ERIC. What is it.

MELANIE. You know who's dying to do this? *(Meaning the script.)*

ERIC. Who?

MELANIE. Guess.

ERIC. I have no idea.

MELANIE. *(A beat, for effect.) Tyler Shaw.*

ERIC. Who?

MELANIE. Tyler Shaw. *(He looks blank.) Outlaw Billy?* *(He shrugs.)* You don't know *Outlaw Billy*?

ERIC. Sorry.

MELANIE. It's the hour-long hit of the season. On Fox. Billy the Kid, but very "now," very sexy?

ERIC. Of course: *Outlaw Billy*.

MELANIE. Tyler IS *Outlaw Billy*. He IS the show. He's been on the cover of *ev*erything lately; I'm sure you've seen him.

ERIC. How do you know he's interested?

MELANIE. Bernie Glickman called me. Do you know Bernie? *(He shakes his head.)* One of the old-time agents. I *adore* him. I'll introduce you; he's like a character from one of your books; you'll love him. Anyway, Tyler just finished this big action movie that's going to be *huge* and Bernie says he's got like a gazillion offers — and he's turning down *every single one of them!* You know what he told Bernie he wants his next movie to be? *Brooklyn Boy*!

ERIC. Really.

MELANIE. Isn't that fabulous?

ERIC. On the basis of what?

MELANIE. On the basis of, *I* don't know, *you,* the *book,* it's a fabulous part! All I know is he *loves* you.

ERIC. Outlaw Billy loves me? Gee. Can he act?

MELANIE. Oh my God! He's fantastic! I'll get Caitlin to send you a tape. You'll see: He's one of those actors you can't take your eyes off of. Like the young Brando. Or Monty Clift. The camera *adores* him.

ERIC. Huh.

MELANIE. This kid can get our movie made. The studio's dying to work with him. He has a meeting on the lot; he may stop by, he's dying to meet you.

ERIC. Oh, really he — ?

MELANIE. *(The phone rings; she cuts him off.)* This I have to take. *(Into the phone; brusquely.)* What they say? Oh, that is such a — What?! *Fuck them.* That is such a crock of sh — They did not, Jerry, *they never did.* I don't give a *shit* they were in Ojai. What kind of people don't check their voicemail? You know, I don't have time for this. I don't give a shit *what* you do, I want you to fix this. *Fix* it, Jerry, you're our lawyer, what the fuck are we paying you for?! *(Hangs up; to Eric.)* Don't ask. We're building an addition and our neighbors are being unbelievable assholes. You ever renovate?

ERIC. No.

MELANIE. Uch. You are so lucky. It is such a nightmare; we should've just *moved.*

ERIC. *(Refers to his watch.)* You know, Melanie, I hate to do this but I have to catch an earlier flight …

MELANIE. *(Over " … earlier flight … ")* Yes yes yes. The script. This fabulous script.

ERIC. So you're happy with it?

MELANIE. Oh, yes, *very* happy.

ERIC. Good. I couldn't tell.

MELANIE. I'm ecstatic. I'm *thrilled.*

ERIC. That's a relief. I thought maybe you were disappointed.

MELANIE. No! It's great, Eric. You did a terrific job. An *amazing* job. It's a great first draft.

ERIC. *(A beat.)* Thank you.

MELANIE. Your characters! Your dialogue! Were you bugging my family all these years? *(He chuckles.)* The father?! That was *my* father!

ERIC. Yours, too, huh?

MELANIE. The *writing,* Eric — the way it's *written;* the *quality* — is such a pleasure, I can't tell you. You don't *read* writing like this.

ERIC. Thank you.

MELANIE. It's so good, you don't want to touch a thing. Not a word. But before we show it to the studio, there are a few little tweaks here and there.

ERIC. Of course.

MELANIE. We made you a copy of this … *(Hands him a stapled report.)*

ERIC. Your notes?

MELANIE. Mine and Caitlin's, uh-huh.

ERIC. Caitlin, the assistant you were going to send out for salad?

MELANIE. She's incredibly smart. Fresh out of *Yale.*

ERIC. Uh-huh.

MELANIE. First of all, it's a little long.

ERIC. I know; I tried to keep it down.

MELANIE. I know you did.

ERIC. There's so much I had to leave out.

MELANIE. I know! With material this good, you have to be ruthless! It's painful, I know.

ERIC. How much do we have to lose?

MELANIE. Thirty pages.

ERIC. *Thirty?*

MELANIE. A *good* thirty. If it was formatted correctly, you naughty boy, it would've run more like 150, so at *least* thirty.

ERIC. *(Over " … so at least … ")* Was it that obvious?!

MELANIE. You were running long so you cheated the margins and reduced the font size.

ERIC. You're *good.*

MELANIE. Hey. I've seen it all. *(Back to the notes.)* Now, as much as I hate to say it, some of those dialogue scenes are going to have to come down.

ERIC. I thought you loved the dialogue.

MELANIE. I do! I hate doing this as much as *you* do! But if they see those seven/eight-page dialogue scenes…!

ERIC. Audiences can't stay glued to a scene for five minutes?

MELANIE. No. They really can't. *(Back to the notes.)* Now: My Big Note — and it was really weird, Caitlin had the exact same note —

ERIC. Uh-huh.

MELANIE. *(Continuous.)* My biggest note is about content.

ERIC. Content.

MELANIE. Yeah. Right now the script is a little too … How shall I put it? A touch too ethnic.

ERIC. Too ethnic? *(She nods.)* The Fleischmans are Jewish.

MELANIE. Of course they are.

ERIC. That's not a new development; they've always been Jewish. They're a *Jewish* family. Remember?

52

MELANIE. *(Over "They're ... ")* Hey, I'm Jewish, too, bubbie; I'm a nice Jewish girl from Long Island. But it's one thing to be Jewish in a *book,* and another to be Jewish in a *movie.*

ERIC. And how is that.

MELANIE. In a movie you're *seeing* them.

ERIC. Yeah? ...

MELANIE. They're right *there,* in front of you. There's nothing *imaginary* about them. Imagining Jews is much easier than actually seeing them.

ERIC. Easier for whom?

MELANIE. For most of the world. You have to think like an average moviegoer. Or a studio executive, for that matter. Think about what they're seeing, how it looks to them. How's the studio going to *sell* this movie? Who are they going to get to *see* it? What are *those* people going to tell their friends about this movie with all these *Jews* running around? That's why I think it would be wise not to make it quite so in-your-face Jewish.

ERIC. "In-your-face"?!

MELANIE. Yes.

ERIC. I don't get it. Why is this suddenly an issue when it's always been there?

MELANIE. *(Over " ... when it's ... ")* Darlin', do you want to get your movie made? 'Cause if you don't ... *(Shrugs.)* that's up to you. I've been producing movies a long time; you're just gonna have to trust me.

ERIC. Is this your concern or the studio's?

MELANIE. I know what freaks them out.

ERIC. Did the studio actually *read* the book? ...

MELANIE. Eric, darlin', *they're* the ones bankrolling your movie!

ERIC. But you're talking about pandering!

MELANIE. No, no. It's a very delicate thing you're trying to do here; you have to be very careful about this. You're talking about putting a relatively small segment of the population out there as mass entertainment. Let's face it, Jews are exotic to most of the planet, and frankly some people could care less about Jews.

ERIC. What about *Schindler's List*?!

MELANIE. Righteous Gentile. Jew As Victim. You can get away with that. Besides, who even REMEMBERS *Schindler's List*? It's old news. Look, the studio didn't buy your book because it's a wonderful novel about a Jewish family. Let's get real. They bought it because it's a great coming-of-age story they think they can market and generate substantial profits from.

ERIC. You're asking me to *extract* the Jewishness and expect it to be the same story?

MELANIE. *(Over " … and expect it … ")* I'm not asking you to *extract* it, darlin', I never said that. All I'm saying is: Tone it down. For your own good. Lower the Jewish Quotient.

ERIC. And how would you propose I do that?

MELANIE. *(Flips through the script.)* Everybody's Jewish! What if you had a non-Jewish character? His friend. That nerdy kid.

ERIC. Seth Bernstein?

MELANIE. Yeah. Does he have to be Jewish?

ERIC. Does Seth *Bernstein* have to be Jewish?

MELANIE. You know what I'm saying: Couldn't he be black?

ERIC. Make Seth Bernstein black?

MELANIE. So you change his name.

ERIC. The Jewishness is integral to the story! It's about a place and a people, and the effect of a place *on* a people! You can't just mix-and-match like this. It's insane!

MELANIE. *(Over "It's insane!")* Bubbie, be open-minded … *(Tyler Shaw — tall, blond, surfer-boy handsome; satchel, sunglasses, the whole bit — enters confidently.)*

TYLER. *(Jocularly.)* All right, break it up you two …

MELANIE. Look who's here!

TYLER. Melanie! *(He dips her back and kisses her while Eric waits awkwardly to be acknowledged.)* You look great!

MELANIE. So do you!

TYLER. *(To Eric.)* Hi, I'm Tyler.

MELANIE. *(Introducing.)* Tyler, this is Eric Weiss.

ERIC. *(Over " … Eric Weiss.")* Hello. *(They shake hands.)*

TYLER. Wow. What an honor, sir. Really.

ERIC. *(Over "Really.")* Nice to meet *you*, too.

TYLER. Shit, are my cheeks red? They always get red whenever I get nervous. I have like such awe for writers.

MELANIE. *(To Eric.)* I *told* you he was crazy about you.

TYLER. How you guys have the discipline to sit down and write page after page! … Stephen King? Oh, man! You ever read *IT*?

ERIC. No, I never have.

TYLER. *(Over "I never have.")* It's like *this* thick. *(Indicates a long tome.)* Longest book I ever read in my life. Took like months.

ERIC. Uh-huh.

MELANIE. *(To Tyler.)* I was just telling Eric how much you love

Brooklyn Boy.

TYLER. Oh, man!

ERIC. Thank you. I'm glad.

MELANIE. Isn't it fabulous?!

TYLER. I didn't actually read the book?

ERIC. No?

TYLER. I read the coverage?

ERIC. Uh-huh.

TYLER. I read the *screenplay* though. Lots of times. But I'm reading it now. Bernie — my agent? — he wants me to do a part that really lets me show my range and get out of the teen-idol trap? This is perfect. I get to age from like twelve to twenty-two. And play against type? They love it when you play against type. *(He laughs; a beat; self-consciously, to Eric.)* What.

ERIC. Hm?

TYLER. *(To Melanie.)* Uh-oh. He's looking at my hair.

ERIC. What?

MELANIE. He says you're looking at his hair.

ERIC. No I'm not.

TYLER. You're thinking: This WASPy guy wants to play Kenny Fleeshman?! No way.

ERIC. *(Correcting him.)* Fleischman.

TYLER. What?

ERIC. Kenny Fleischman.

TYLER. Fleischman? Sorry. I just want to assure you, sir: these highlights? They're gone; they're history. I'm going *dark* for this; *you* know, like dark brown?

MELANIE. *(With intense interest.)* Uh-huh, uh-huh.

TYLER. I already talked to my hair guy? Miguel, the guy who does my hair for *everything?* He was thinking maybe like a curly perm?

MELANIE. Or a slight wave?

TYLER. Yeah. Exactly. To make me look more … *you* know.

MELANIE. *(To Eric.)* He could pass. Don't you think? With darker hair?

TYLER. I always find my characters through my hair. Always. It's like once I get the right hair, I *become* them. This movie I just did? My character was supposed to be like this bipolar, futuristic, hip-hop deejay, bounty-hunter guy?

ERIC. Uh-huh.

TYLER. Miguel gave me this really radical buzz cut? The minute I saw myself in the mirror, it was like, "Yeah! All right! *Now* I get it."

ERIC. Uh-huh.

TYLER. And don't worry. *(To Melanie.)* He looks so worried! *(To Eric.)* I won't be so buff, I promise. I had to be really ripped for this movie — abs, chest, arms — I bulked up big time. *Killed* myself, I was like on zero fat for six months.

MELANIE. Oh my God.

TYLER. I was starving.

MELANIE. Poor thing!

TYLER. *(Continuous.)* Now I'm working with a trainer and a nutritionist to *lose* all the muscle mass I killed myself to put on? 'Cause Kenny's got to be soft. You know? He's *gotta* be. Not flabby, but soft. Like a typical Jewish boy.

ERIC. Uh-huh.

TYLER. I'm working with this awesome dialect coach on my Brooklyn accent?

MELANIE. Oh, isn't that fabulous!

TYLER. *(Deliberately bad accent.)* I wanna sound fuckin' aut'entic, like Tony Manero in *Saturday Night Fever. (Melanie laughs; Eric doesn't.)* I'm kidding! *(To Melanie.)* He's so serious! *(To Eric.)* I had my assistant order me all these books on being Jewish? Jewish history — like a huge box of them. I love research! I love it! I'd love to hang out with *you* sometime.

ERIC. With me?

TYLER. Yeah. To *you* know, pick up your mannerisms and stuff?

MELANIE. What a great idea!

TYLER. The way you put your hand on your mouth and stuff? *(Imitates Eric's gestures.)*

MELANIE. *(Laughing.)* That's hysterical!

ERIC. *(Annoyed.)* Okay, okay.

MELANIE. He's just having fun.

TYLER. *(Over " … having fun.")* Sorry, man. No offense. It's just, I want to do you proud. You know? I want to get everything right, like down to the smallest detail. I mean, it's your story, right? Isn't he supposed to be you?

ERIC. Who.

TYLER. Kenny Fleeshman.

ERIC. Fleischman.

TYLER. Oh, right. I thought he was supposed to be *you*.

ERIC. *(Pointedly.)* No. There *is* no Kenny Fleischman. He doesn't exist. He never existed. I created him.

MELANIE. *(Seeing he's losing his cool; gently.)* Darlin' …

56

TYLER. Hey, look, man, it's such a great part, I want to do it justice. I want you to be happy.

ERIC. *(Surprised.)* You do?

TYLER. Yeah. Of course.

ERIC. You want *my* approval?

TYLER. Yes!

ERIC. That's … really quite endearing, Tyler; thank you. But it doesn't really matter what *I* think; I'm only the writer.

MELANIE. Eric …

ERIC. This reminds me of the joke about the Polish starlet in Hollywood — you know that one? She slept with the writer. *(Eric laughs manically.)*

TYLER. Look. Sir. Maybe I'm not what you saw in your head when you wrote your book. But I "get" this kid. I can play him. I can *become* him. I'll *show* you; I've been working with my coach … *(Takes a scrawled-upon script from his satchel.)*

ERIC. What are you doing?

TYLER. I'll *read* for you.

ERIC. You really don't have to …

MELANIE. Would you? I would love it!

TYLER. I have no problem reading for you … *(Finds a scene.)*

ERIC. You've already proved how passionate you are.

MELANIE. *(To Eric; over "… you are.")* Let him. I think it would be *great* to hear him read it.

TYLER. How about the scene with the father in the barbershop right before Kenny leaves for college?

MELANIE. Oooh, yes! Good choice! I love that scene!

TYLER. Page 128.

MELANIE. 128? *(Finds the page in her script.)*

TYLER. *(To Eric.)* You mind reading with me?

ERIC. Me?

MELANIE. Oh, that is a brilliant idea.

ERIC. Oh no no no.

TYLER. Oh, man, it would be so cool!

ERIC. I'd rather not.

MELANIE. Oh, come on …

ERIC. No, I really don't feel comfortable doing it.

MELANIE. You read in front of large groups of people all the time!

ERIC. This isn't the same.

MELANIE. Don't even think about it, just do it!

TYLER. *(Reads dialogue from the script, as "Kenny")* "Dad?"

MELANIE. *(Reads stage direction from the script.)* "Arnie, seated in a barber chair, looks up from his newspaper and sees Kenny." *(Shows Eric the place in the script. Prompting him.)* "Well, look who's here." *(Eric resists, she eggs him on, he acquiesces. Tyler proves himself to be a surprisingly effective actor.)*

ERIC. *(As "Arnie.")* "Well, look who's here."

TYLER. "Hi."

ERIC. "I thought you already left."

TYLER. "Not yet. My ride should be here any minute."

ERIC. "Who's taking you?"

TYLER. "Car service."

ERIC. "If I didn't have these trims coming in ... "

TYLER. "I know; that's okay." *(A beat.)*

ERIC. "So? What can I do for you?"

TYLER. "I wanted to see you before I left."

ERIC. "You wanted to see *me?*"

TYLER. "Yes."

ERIC. "What for?"

TYLER. "To say goodbye."

ERIC. "You mean you're *talking* to me?"

TYLER. "Of course I'm talking to you. Why wouldn't I be talking to you?"

ERIC. "I don't know, the way you yelled at me last night ... "

TYLER. "That wasn't yelling."

ERIC. "It wasn't? It sure sounded like yelling to *me* ... "

TYLER. "I'm sorry if that's how it sounded. I was frustrated. I was trying to get you to understand. Dad? ... I know you're upset about my going away."

ERIC. "Who says I'm upset?"

TYLER. "I can tell."

ERIC. "You think you know everything? Well, you're wrong. I don't care what you do, you can do whatever the hell you want."

MELANIE. "Outside, a car horn honks. Kenny opens the door and shouts."

TYLER. *(Shouts.)* "I'll be right there!"

ERIC. "Go. You don't want to hit traffic."

TYLER. "Dad, wish me good luck."

ERIC. "There was just a thing in the paper, the potholes on the Van Wyck are unbelievable. Tell the guy who's driving to take it easy."

TYLER. "I will."

ERIC. "You hit a pothole at eighty miles an hour, that's all it takes."

TYLER. *"Dad? Wish me luck. Just say it. That's all I want to hear."*
ERIC. *"What do you need* me *wishing you luck for?"*
TYLER. *"I need to know you wish me well."*
ERIC. *"All of a sudden you care what I think?"*
MELANIE. *"The driver hits the horn."*
ERIC. *"You'd better go."*
TYLER. *"Dad. Please. Just say it."*
MELANIE. *"The horn blares again."*
TYLER. *(Shouts.)* *"Christ! I said I'd be right there!"*
ERIC. *"Go. You don't want to make him mad; it'll affect his driving."*
TYLER. *"Dad? … "*
ERIC. *"How much cash you got?"*
TYLER. *"I've got."*
ERIC. *"Here, take some more."*
TYLER. *"I don't need it."*
ERIC. *"Take, dammit!"*
TYLER. *"Thanks. (A beat.) I'll be back winter break."*
ERIC. *"No you won't."*
TYLER. *"I will."*
ERIC. *"Don't make any promises. Winter's a long way away." (Eric breaks down. Tyler and Melanie are perplexed.)*
MELANIE. Eric? Eric, darlin', you okay?
ERIC. *(Shakes his head, through tears.)* Sorry. *(Eric, sobbing, leaves, as Melanie and Tyler watch him go.)*
TYLER. *(Softly.)* Wow.

Scene 6

Ocean Avenue

The evening of the following day. A middle-class, prewar Brooklyn apartment, decorated with a woman's touch that faded long ago. Cluttered, neglected. A scratchy Sinatra LP plays on the hi-fi. Eric is drinking whiskey and sorting through tchotchkes; packing some, discarding others into a trash bag. He has uncovered several Christmas-wrapped bottles of liquor. The doorbell rings.

ERIC. *(Calls.)* Who is it?
ZIMMER. *(Off.)* Ira. *(Eric turns down the volume.)*
ERIC. Who?
ZIMMER. *(Off.)* Zimmer.
ERIC. *(Winces, then calls.)* One second! *(He braces himself before admitting Zimmer, who enters holding a bakery box.)* Ira. Hello.
ZIMMER. *(Over "Hello.")* Hope you don't mind my coming over.
ERIC. *(Over " … my coming over.")* No no.
ZIMMER. You feel like company, yes or no?
ERIC. Sure. Come in.
ZIMMER. *(Kisses the mezuzah on the doorway as he enters.)* I heard. *(Eric nods.)* Went to the hospital to see my mom? Dropped by your dad's room, just to, *you* know, say hello, see how he was doing? Some other guy was in his bed. An old Chinese guy. The minute I saw that … *(A beat.)* I brought you some rugelach.
ERIC. Oh. Thanks.
ZIMMER. The door's supposed to be left open at a shiva house.
ERIC. I know. I'm not sitting shiva. My *aunt* is. Up in Riverdale.
ZIMMER. *(Nods, then.)* So what happened? At the end.
ERIC. Sepsis. Apparently he went very fast.
ZIMMER. Well, *that's* a blessing, isn't it? Could've been a lot worse. Were you there?
ERIC. *(Shakes his head.)* California.
ZIMMER. Oh, right. Today was the funeral?
ERIC. *(Nods.)* Two o'clock.

60

ZIMMER. Gee, if I'd known … I could've been there …

ERIC. *(Over "I could've … ")* That's all right.

ZIMMER. *(A beat.)* Really sorry, Ricky.

ERIC. *(Over " … Ricky.")* I know.

ZIMMER. Your dad was a real character.

ERIC. Yeah. He was. *(A beat.)* Want some? *(Meaning Canadian Club.)*

ZIMMER. You drink that stuff?

ERIC. No. But it's here. And drinking seems to be in order.

ZIMMER. Yeah, I'll have a little with you, why not. This much. *(Eric hands him a glass; Zimmer toasts.) L'chaim.*

ERIC. *L'chaim. (They drink.)* You see all this? All this hard liquor? The joke is: The man didn't drink. At all. Grape juice at Passover. He just liked to collect gifts from customers. There must be thirty years of booze stacked up in the closet, still in Christmas boxes. Help yourself.

ZIMMER. Nah.

ERIC. Take. However many you like.

ZIMMER. Seriously? *I'm* not a *shikka,* either.

ERIC. What am *I* gonna do with all this?

ZIMMER. Okay. Sure, I'll take some off your hands. Thanks. *(A beat.)* You mind if I…? *(Meaning open the pastry box.)*

ERIC. Go ahead.

ZIMMER. *(Eating.)* These are really good. *(Looks around the cluttered room.) Look* at all this stuff.

ERIC. I've been at it for hours and I haven't made a dent. The stuff he accumulated since my mother died! The guy was a QVC addict. Who knew?

ZIMMER. What are you trying to do?

ERIC. I've got to pack this place up.

ZIMMER. *Now?* What are you in such a hurry for?

ERIC. It has to be done, eventually.

ZIMMER. Give yourself a break. You shouldn't be doing this now.

ERIC. I don't know what to do with myself. I need to do *some*-thing. I certainly didn't want to go up to Riverdale — that would've been a different kind of hell. And the prospect of going home to an empty apartment …

ZIMMER. Why empty? Where's your wife?

ERIC. What wife?

ZIMMER. What do you mean, "What wife?"

ERIC. I got my own place. She wants a divorce.

ZIMMER. Since when? *(Eric gestures, "Don't ask.")* So on top of everything, you're *alone? (Eric nods.)* Ya know? Shiva's been practiced for thousands of years for a very good reason. If there's one thing Jews are good at, it's grief. You're supposed to let friends comfort you, bring you food, help you heal.

ERIC. Thank you, Rabbi.

ZIMMER. *(A beat.)* Ricky. The other day. At the hospital. I'm sorry we had a fight.

ERIC. We didn't have a fight.

ZIMMER. Yes we did. I hate fighting with my friends. Ask Mindy. I've been eating my *kishkes* out, waking up in the middle of the night. Seeing you again? After so long? All this *dreck* came backing up. My father and stuff? My *life?* Little things like that.

ERIC. I know what you mean.

ZIMMER. Yeah? *(Eric nods. Pause. Zimmer looks around the room.)* I remember watching TV here. Your mother sitting there smoking.

ERIC. Like a chimney.

ZIMMER. Eating over. I first had Mott's apple-cranberry sauce at your house.

ERIC. Is that a fact.

ZIMMER. You don't forget a thing like that. I thought that was the coolest thing in the world. Who would've thought of mixing the two together? I made my mother get it.

ERIC. Do they still make it?

ZIMMER. I don't know. *(Silence.)* So, all the moms and dads'll be gone soon, huh, Ricky.

ERIC. Yup. All of 'em.

ZIMMER. Yup. *(Pause.)* So how was L.A.?

ERIC. Not so great.

ZIMMER. Why? What happened?

ERIC. I'm off the movie.

ZIMMER. What does that mean?

ERIC. I asked to be taken off the movie. They're replacing me. Hiring another screenwriter.

ZIMMER. On your own book?! Can they do that?

ERIC. Yes.

ZIMMER. But it's your book!

ERIC. Yes, but I sold them the rights.

ZIMMER. Can't you take it back or something?

ERIC. No. It's theirs now. They paid me for it.

ZIMMER. What if you gave them their money back?

ERIC. I can't. It's already spent. It went toward the down payment on my new apartment.

ZIMMER. So, this doesn't mean the movie's not gonna get made, does it?

ERIC. No.

ZIMMER. Good!

ERIC. It just means that if it *does* get made, I won't have anything to do with it.

ZIMMER. Aren't you upset? It's your baby!

ERIC. To tell you the truth, I'm actually relieved. *(A beat.)* Lately I feel as if I've been trying on a whole new wardrobe, none of which feels … authentic. *(A confession.)* The other night in L.A.? After my book signing?

ZIMMER. Yeah…?

ERIC. I took a girl back to my hotel with me.

ZIMMER. You did? *(Eric nods.)* A girl? *(Eric nods. A beat.)* How old?

ERIC. You don't want to know.

ZIMMER. Yes I do.

ERIC. Well, I'm not telling you.

ZIMMER. *That* young? Uy uy uy. *(A beat.)* Is that why your wife is leaving you? Because of this girl?

ERIC. *(Over "Because … ")* No, no; we've been in trouble for a long time. I'd never done anything like that in my life. The situation presented itself and I thought I'd try it on, like a new coat. *(A beat.)* I'd just gotten the call about my dad and the truth is I didn't want to be alone. *(Pause.)*

ZIMMER. Ricky. I want to help you.

ERIC. What do you mean, "help" me?

ZIMMER. You're suffering. I see you suffering like this …

ERIC. My father just died.

ZIMMER. I don't mean just now. The other day, when I ran into you. There was something in your eyes — a sadness.

ERIC. "A sadness."

ZIMMER. Yeah. A light is gone from your eyes, Ricky. You can't hide it from me. I know the real you. I'm your oldest friend. I know you longer than anybody.

ERIC. Ira, we were friends a long time ago. There's been a gap of *twenty-five* years. Quarter of a century, Ira. That's not the same as being my oldest friend. *(Zimmer reaches into his pocket and takes out a yarmulke.)*

ZIMMER. Say Kaddish with me.

ERIC. No.

ZIMMER. I'll say it *with* you. *(Takes a piece of paper from his pocket.)* I wrote it out phonetically for you.

ERIC. Stop trying to convert me! Jesus, you're like one of those mitzvah-mobile guys!

ZIMMER. What is the big deal? You say a prayer for the dead, what do you think'll happen to you?

ERIC. I'm not interested.

ZIMMER. It might actually make you feel better. Don't you want to feel better?

ERIC. Judaism has *never* helped me feel better. I've always found it sorrowful, guilt-provoking. There was never any comfort. Not for me.

ZIMMER. Maybe that's how it seemed when we were in Hebrew school, but not anymore. We have this wonderful congregation now, this terrific young rabbi …

ERIC. Good.

ZIMMER. *(Continuous.)* I'd love to take you to talk to him.

ERIC. Look. Ira. Whatever works for you. I wouldn't presume to impose my beliefs — not on you, not on anybody.

ZIMMER. *(Over " … not on anybody.")* What *are* your beliefs? Huh? What do you believe in?

ERIC. What do I believe in? I believe in survival. Organisms make choices in order to survive. I chose to *escape* from all this; you chose to stay. Fine!

ZIMMER. *(Over "Fine!")* You talk about escape from Brooklyn like it's Treblinka or something! It's not the worst place in the world!

ERIC. I'm not saying it is.

ZIMMER. *(Continuous.)* I live here! It's my home!

ERIC. I know! But this is *my* Brooklyn. This apartment. Whatever's left for me of Brooklyn is right here. And it'll be shipped off to Goodwill soon enough. *(Pause.)*

ZIMMER. Ricky, Kaddish isn't about death.

ERIC. Ira …

ZIMMER. *(Continuous.)* It's about reaffirming life. Why don't you just *try* it with me? *(Offers the yarmulke.)* Do it for your dad. *Yis'ga'dal v'yis'kadash* — *(Eric throws the yarmulke to the floor. Pause. Zimmer picks it up and kisses it. Silence.)* Well. *(Makes motions toward leaving.)* If you ever have a change of heart … you know where to find me.

ERIC. 1911 Avenue X.

ZIMMER. *(Nods, remembers the offer of liquor.)* You sure you don't mind if I, uh …

ERIC. Help yourself. *(Silence as he watches Zimmer select boxes of liquor.)* Ira? You were right.

ZIMMER. About what?

ERIC. He's you.

ZIMMER. What?

ERIC. Seth Bernstein is you.

ZIMMER. *(Pleased.)* He *is*? *(Eric nods.)* He *is*? *(Eric nods again.)* I knew it!

ERIC. Thanks for the shiva call.

ZIMMER. Don't mention it.

ERIC. *(A beat.)* So long, Ira.

ZIMMER. *(Nods, then:)* Zy'gezunt. *(Zimmer exits. Eric resumes packing. He roughly tosses QVC gadgets, still in their original packaging, into a box.)*

ERIC. *Look* at this crap … *Look* at this … *(Manny appears, looking healthy, dressed in clothes typical of what he wore in life.)*

MANNY. Easy, with that! You don't want to *break* it …

ERIC. What the hell were you *think*ing?

MANNY. *(Shrugs.)* You never know when you might need something. *(At the bookcase.)* Look at all the *books* your mother had! Anything Jewish. *Marjorie Morningstar.* She loved *Marjorie Morningstar.* Leon Uris. *Exodus, Mila 18.* Always with the books. You got it from her. I read maybe a couple start to finish the last fifty years.

ERIC. Yeah? What.

MANNY. *My Gun is Quick.* Mickey Spillane. Excellent book. *I, the Jury.* The follow-up. I liked that too. Henry Miller. *Nexus, Plexus, Sexus?* Remember those?

ERIC. Uh-huh.

MANNY. *(Continuous.)* The books that were banned in Boston? I didn't read the whole books, though, just the dirty parts. And, boy, were they dirty! Filthy! Some of the stuff he had going on in there! *(Whistles.)* Unbelievable! I kept them hidden in my night table.

ERIC. I *know;* I found them.

MANNY. Son of a gun! *(A beat.)* Your mother's been dead *how* long?, thirty-odd years? You'd think a man all alone, pacing these four and a half rooms, books and books all around, might one day pick one up to see what was inside — out of curiosity, if nothing else. But, no. Not me. Not once.

ERIC. That's an amazing feat, Dad. How'd you manage that?

MANNY. It wasn't easy.

ERIC. What was it, one more way of getting back at me?

MANNY. You scared the shit out of me! From the first words you read out loud — you were like not yet four, I knew I was in big trouble. Thank God I had the store; I was the smartest guy in the world in that store. I had those shoeboxes arranged perfectly, in size order. I needed to be the master of *some*thing, for crissake, why not shoes? At least they don't talk back. *(A beat.)* You know, simple men may not have the talent for words and ideas that some men have, but don't assume there's nothing going on behind the silence and the sarcasm. There's plenty.

ERIC. Like what?

MANNY. Oh, a kind of terror. That's all. Resentment. That sort of thing. Embarrassment. Shame.

ERIC. Why shame?

MANNY. Why? Because a *husband* should be first in the eyes of his wife, not the son, *that's* why shame.

ERIC. She loved you, Dad.

MANNY. I know that; you don't have to tell me that. But let's not kid ourselves, *boychik,* she *adored* you. You came in first; I only placed. It's not natural when the son wins. It leaves the poor schmuck father out in the cold and that makes him mad. And for the son? It's very confusing. Look what it did to *you.*

ERIC. *What* did it do to me. I think I did pretty well considering the years of psychological abuse heaped on me by my father.

MANNY. Let me ask you this: Was that such a bad thing?

ERIC. What?!

MANNY. I gave you something to write about. If everything was hunky-dory, you'd be just another Brooklyn boy with no particular stories to tell. Would you have a critically acclaimed autobiographical novel on the best-seller list? I don't think so.

ERIC. So, let me see if I've got this straight: I'm supposed to be *grateful* to you for belittling me my entire life?

MANNY. *(Shrugs.)* Think about it: You had your mother thinking your shit was gold and I, who made a point of telling you it stank like everybody else's. *Two* adoring parents would've been overkill.

ERIC. *(Skeptical.)* So you were doing me a favor.

MANNY. Basically.

ERIC. Huh.

MANNY. *(A beat.)* Oh, I read your book, by the way.

ERIC. You did?

MANNY. Uh-huh.

ERIC. All of it?

MANNY. Yeah. Why? You surprised?

ERIC. Well, yeah. I assumed you didn't get a chance to read it.

MANNY. I started after you left and I couldn't put it down. I stayed up all that night and into the morning before the sepsis hit.

ERIC. So what are you telling me? My book killed you? Great.

MANNY. *(Laughs.)* No no no. *(A beat.)* I liked it.

ERIC. You did? *(Manny nods.)* Really?

MANNY. I really did. It's a good book you wrote, Ricky.

ERIC. *(Pleasantly surprised.)* Thanks, Dad.

MANNY. You sure were paying attention all those years. You've got everything in there. I laughed, I cried. It all came back to me. Everything. Our whole lives. *(A beat.)* You did good.

ERIC. Thanks.

MANNY. *(A beat.)* How do you do it?

ERIC. Do what?

MANNY. How do you sit down and build something out of words, something that wasn't there before?

ERIC. *(Shrugs.)* I invent. And imagine. And remember.

MANNY. Yeah? And then somehow you put it into words?

ERIC. *(Nods.)* Yeah.

MANNY. *I* could never do that. I wouldn't know where to begin. Must be a great thing to be able to do.

ERIC. It is. *(Pause.)* Dad? Why couldn't we talk like this when you were alive?

MANNY. *(Shrugs.)* Life isn't like this. *(A beat.)* Ah, it's just as well. You wouldn't be you if we did; you'd be somebody else. An accountant or something. *(Eric laughs. Manny recedes into the shadows. Silence. Eric turns on the TV. A ball game. He comes upon the paper Zimmer left behind on which Kaddish is written. Experimentally, he begins to read, haltingly at first, his voice becoming more confident as he proceeds.)*

ERIC. *Yis'ga'dal v'yis'kadash sh'may ra'bbo, b'olmo dee'vro chir'usay v'yamlich malchu'say, b'chayaychon uv'yomay'chon uv'chayay d'chol bai Yisroel, ba'agolo u'viz'man koriv; v'imru Omein …* (Lights fade.)

End of Play

PROPERTY LIST

Book, papers, coat, umbrella (ERIC)
Orange (ERIC)
Glasses (MANNY)
Coffee, cell phone (ERIC)
Coffee, cake, newspaper (IRA)
Wallet (IRA)
Shopping bag with Chinese takeout (ERIC)
Galleys (NINA)
Box of books, CDs, LPs, sweater (NINA)
Stack of mail (NINA)
Keys (ERIC)
Minibar food, bottles of water (ALISON)
Book (ALISON)
Bottle of water (ERIC)
Scripts, notes (MELANIE)
Bottles of whiskey, liquor (ERIC)
Boxes, packing material (ERIC)
Bakery box (IRA)
Yarmulke, paper (IRA)

SOUND EFFECTS

Hospital sounds
TV movie soundtrack
Toilet flush
Phone ring
Sinatra album
Ball game

NEW PLAYS

★ **INTIMATE APPAREL by Lynn Nottage.** The moving and lyrical story of a turn-of-the-century black seamstress whose gifted hands and sewing machine are the tools she uses to fashion her dreams from the whole cloth of her life's experiences. "…Nottage's play has a delicacy and eloquence that seem absolutely right for the time she is depicting…" *–NY Daily News.* "…thoughtful, affecting…The play offers poignant commentary on an era when the cut and color of one's dress—and of course, skin—determined whom one could and could not marry, sleep with, even talk to in public." *–Variety.* [2M, 4W] ISBN: 0-8222-2009-1

★ **BROOKLYN BOY by Donald Margulies.** A witty and insightful look at what happens to a writer when his novel hits the bestseller list. "The characters are beautifully drawn, the dialogue sparkles…" *–nytheatre.com.* "Few playwrights have the mastery to smartly investigate so much through a laugh-out-loud comedy that combines the vintage subject matter of successful writer-returning-to-ethnic-roots with the familiar mid-life crisis." *–Show Business Weekly.* [4M, 3W] ISBN: 0-8222-2074-1

★ **CROWNS by Regina Taylor.** Hats become a springboard for an exploration of black history and identity in this celebratory musical play. "Taylor pulls off a Hat Trick: She scores thrice, turning CROWNS into an artful amalgamation of oral history, fashion show, and musical theater…" *–TheatreMania.com.* "…wholly theatrical…Ms. Taylor has created a show that seems to arise out of spontaneous combustion, as if a bevy of department-store customers simultaneously decided to stage a revival meeting in the changing room." *–NY Times.* [1M, 6W (2 musicians)] ISBN: 0-8222-1963-8

★ **EXITS AND ENTRANCES by Athol Fugard.** The story of a relationship between a young playwright on the threshold of his career and an aging actor who has reached the end of his. "[Fugard] can say more with a single line than most playwrights convey in an entire script…Paraphrasing the title, it's safe to say this drama, making its memorable entrance into our consciousness, is unlikely to exit as long as a theater exists for exceptional work." *–Variety.* "A thought-provoking, elegant and engrossing new play…" *–Hollywood Reporter.* [2M] ISBN: 0-8222-2041-5

★ **BUG by Tracy Letts.** A thriller featuring a pair of star-crossed lovers in an Oklahoma City motel facing a bug invasion, paranoia, conspiracy theories and twisted psychological motives. "…obscenely exciting…top-flight craftsmanship. Buckle up and brace yourself…" *–NY Times.* "…[a] thoroughly outrageous and thoroughly entertaining play…the possibility of enemies, real and imagined, to squash has never been more theatrical." *–A.P.* [3M, 2W] ISBN: 0-8222-2016-4

★ **THOM PAIN (BASED ON NOTHING) by Will Eno.** An ordinary man muses on childhood, yearning, disappointment and loss, as he draws the audience into his last-ditch plea for empathy and enlightenment. "It's one of those treasured nights in the theater—treasured nights anywhere, for that matter—that can leave you both breathless with exhilaration and…in a puddle of tears." *–NY Times.* "Eno's words…are familiar, but proffered in a way that is constantly contradictory to our expectations. Beckett is certainly among his literary ancestors." *–nytheatre.com.* [1M] ISBN: 0-8222-2076-8

★ **THE LONG CHRISTMAS RIDE HOME by Paula Vogel.** Past, present and future collide on a snowy Christmas Eve for a troubled family of five. "…[a] lovely and hauntingly original family drama…a work that breathes so much life into the theater." *–Time Out.* "…[a] delicate visual feast…" *–NY Times.* "…brutal and lovely…the overall effect is magical." *–NY Newsday.* [3M, 3W] ISBN: 0-8222-2003-2

DRAMATISTS PLAY SERVICE, INC.
440 Park Avenue South, New York, NY 10016 212-683-8960 Fax 212-213-1539
postmaster@dramatists.com www.dramatists.com